# Bible Study
## in Blended Ministry Churches*

***Blended Ministry Church:***
*A traditional church operating in two modes. In the traditional mode, the church reaches, teaches, and minsters to people through traditional on-campus programs and ministries. In the non-traditional mode, the church reaches, teaches, and ministers to people in their own cultural setting.*

## by Robert A. Dawson

*Wipf and Stock Publishers*
150 West Broadway • Eugene OR 97401
2001

*This book is dedicated
to every student who values
following Jesus more
than following tradition*

Bible Study in Blended Ministry Churches

By Dawson, Robert A.
Copyright©2001 by Dawson, Robert A.
ISBN: 1-57910-741-9

Printed by <u>*Wipf and Stock Publishers*</u>
*150 West Broadway • Eugene OR 97401*

Unless otherwise stated, all Scripture citations are from
the Holman Christian Study Bible, © 2000 Holman Bible Publishers,
a division of LifeWay Christian Resources, Nashville, Tennessee
Used by permission

# Table of Contents

- Acknowledgments .................................................. iv
- Preface ................................................................ v

## Part 1: Examining Past and Present ........................ 1
- Chapter 1: Sunday School 101 ................................. 3
- Chapter 2: Counting the Cost ................................. 17

## Part 2: Blending Ministries ................................... 31
- Chapter 3: Possibilities for Growth and Ministry ........ 41
- Chapter 4: Organizing for Growth ........................... 57
- Chapter 5: Staffing the Organization ....................... 69
- Chapter 6: Becoming a Team ................................. 93
- Chapter 7: Providing Facilities and Equipment ......... 111

## Part 3: Changing Lives ....................................... 127
- Chapter 8: Using Curriculum, Changing Lives .......... 129
- Chapter 9: Getting to Work: Outreach, Evangelism, and Ministry .... 149

# Acknowledgments

Few books are the product of one individual, and this one is no exception. I am first of all indebted to my own teachers. This is a large and diverse group of individuals, several of whom are with the Lord. They include men such as Arthur Flake, J. N. Barnette, John Sisemore, and Harry Piland. These taught me through their writings writings the principles and methods that have made Sunday School what it is -- a priceless gift of God to Southern Baptists. Others, including Professors LeRoy Ford and Jack Terry, mentored me from the classroom, teaching me about curriculum building and learning processes. All of these mentioned have shown me the value of the Sunday School as a tool for reaching and teaching people. It has been part of my life's work to pass their legacy on to other generations of religious educators.

I am indebted to another group that is quite different from the first. These individuals never earned a seminary doctorate or wrote a book. They are quite remarkable, however. They taught me through their examples that my efforts as a religious educator have not always been turned in the right direction. They showed me a style of ministry that is more like that of Jesus than anything I have known. Included in this list of names are Tillie Burgin, Don Lane, and Charles Davenport. Like Jesus, they have taken Bible study and ministry out of the temples and into the streets. You'll get to know these very Christ-like people and their ministries through the pages of this book. There is one young adult whose name does not appear elsewhere in these pages, but his influence does. My son, Jeremy Dawson, through his own music ministry to street kids and "ravers", was one of the first to show me how very much I was missing the mark.

Another group has been invaluable in the preparation of this manuscript. I wish to offer special thanks to Janet Burns, Secretary to the School of Christian Service at OBU for serving as my preliminary reader and for catching most of the typos. I am further indebted to Francine Roark Robison, friend and partner in missions, for her long hours in editing this work. She taught me more about where commas *don't* belong than any other person I've known. If these pages make any sense at all, it is partly because she read them before you did.

Finally, I want to thank my wife, Alyce, for her quiet and loving support as this book was prepared. My work on this manuscript took me away to the office many times when I could have been at home. Once again, she never complained.

# Preface

*Bible Study in Blended Ministry Churches* was written initially for students in educational ministry classes at Oklahoma Baptist University and for students in OBU's Ministry Training Institute. As a textbook, it provides the Sunday School component for educational ministry classes. Books on Southern Baptist Sunday School work are introduced and then pass from the scene rather quickly. There was a felt need for greater continuity in educational ministry classes. At the same time, there was a need to remember certain lessons from the past to undergird present day efforts. We have tried to include those lessons.

This book is further intended to be a handbook for use by pastors, Christian educators, and Sunday School teachers and officers in traditional Southern Baptist churches. Most of the pages in this volume focus on the traditional approaches that emerged from the foundation laid by Sunday School leaders such as Arthur Flake, J. N. Barnette, and Harry Piland. It is hoped that current church educational leaders, both volunteer and staff, will find new ways of applying these principles.

If these traditional Sunday School approaches were the sole focus of *Bible Study in Blended Ministry Churches*, this volume would hardly be necessary. Many good books on Sunday School principles and their applications have been produced in recent years by LifeWay Christian Resources, formerly known as the Baptist Sunday School Board. The transformational potential of Bible study through the Sunday School has been a helpful and much needed emphasis in works published since 2000. In short, if several good books on Sunday School principles and methods are available, why is *this* book needed?

For part of the answer to that question, let's go back in time fifty years. In 1950, Southern Baptist Sunday School enrollment was 5,024,553. This figure represented approximately 3.3% of the US population of some 152 million. By 1960, Sunday School enrollment had grown to 7,382,550, a net increase of approximately 2.3 million. By that time, approximately 4.1% of the US population of 181 million people was enrolled in Sunday School in Southern Baptist churches. Growth slowed to a virtual halt over the next forty years. By 2000, Sunday School enrollment had reached 8,186,415. This figure represented only 2.9% of the US population of 281 million people. If the rate of growth of 46.9% experienced during the decade of the 1950s had continued to the present time, *Sunday School enrollment would have exceeded 34 million* by 2000, or more than *12%* of the US population.

What accounts for our failure to experience continued growth? We must remember that during the decade of the 1950s, our country had just survived a world war. Many had turned to God during those years. Southern Baptist Sunday Schools were well-positioned in society to provide

Bible instruction for many who were seeking it. Studies reveal that the young and median adults of that decade were predominantly evangelical Christians. It was natural that they would join churches and enroll in Sunday Schools. *Today, if our communities were still populated by white, middle-class evangelical Christians looking for churches to join, our Sunday Schools and churches would still be growing.* Isn't it possible that our churches today *act* as if these people still populated our neighborhoods?

Churches are generally established in new, growing communities filled by people with hopes for a bright future. These are generally the first members of the new congregations. They develop ways of doing ministry that are very comfortable for them. Over the years, however, neighborhoods change and the original members become more affluent. They move out to newer communities and leave houses that become rental property occupied by a low-income, racially mixed population. The church itself seldom changes, though. It's members simply burn more gas getting there. As a result of the failure of many churches to adapt their ministry style to the needs of changing populations and cultures, those who live closest to our churches are sometimes the most overlooked.

This book is based on three fundamental principles. *First,* the solution to reaching people still lies within the local churches and their programs of Bible teaching. We are still the body of Christ, and Christ is always relevant to every person of every culture.

*Second,* our traditional on-campus ministries must be turned outward rather than inward. We must stop regarding our churches and our Sunday School classes as cultural oases within a frightening and threatening landscape. Chapter 2 of this book suggests some costs to be paid by laity and staff alike in reaching people.

*Third,* we must admit honestly that these efforts will *still* not be enough. Even though we become willing to open our doors wider than ever before, some on the outside will still not enter. For those who will not, we must learn to take Bible study to them. This is the very essence of a blended ministry church: A traditional church that does many non-traditional things to reach and teach people in their own cultural settings.

It is for this purpose that *Bible Study in Blended Ministry Churches* was written: to help students, pastors, and lay leaders seek ways to reach and teach more effectively in traditional settings while seeking new and exciting opportunities for non-traditional, off-campus Bible study ministries. As you read these pages, please do not be offended by their content. Rather, prayerfully seek opportunities to be involved in blended ministries.

– *Bob Dawson, August, 2001*

# Part 1:
## Examining Past and Present

**Introduction**

**Chapter 1: Sunday School 101**
- Sunday School beginnings
- Lessons from our history
- Lessons from the present
- What have we learned?

**Chapter 2: Counting the Cost**
- Facing our failures
- The cost to be paid by members
- The cost to be paid by staff
- What are our options?
- The cost of doing nothing

# Introduction to Part 1

Southern Baptists have a rich heritage in the Sunday School. Baptists were among the first to embrace Sunday School and make it an integral part of local churches. With the establishment of the Sunday School Board in 1891, Southern Baptists took the lead in organization, curriculum development, and participation. Sunday School was the key to the growth of the Southern Baptist denomination throughout the twentieth century.

At the dawn of the 21st century, however, many are questioning its effectiveness. Some have called it a dinosaur that could face extinction during the first half of this new century. Several questions must be asked:

1. *Does Sunday School have a biblical and historical place in the ministries of our churches?* After all, churches did without them for almost 18 centuries of Christian history. Can the continued existence of the Sunday School be justified on biblical or historical grounds?

2. *Have Sunday Schools become outmoded as an avenue of church growth?* For the past thirty years, Sunday School has been promoted as the "growth" arm of the church. It is the only program organization with an assigned responsibility for outreach and evangelism. Practically, is that still true? Many pastors today seem to opt for seeker-friendly, contemporary worship services as the means of drawing people in. Many feel that the Sunday School has turned inward toward complacency and ineffectiveness.

3. *Do the traditions of Sunday School render it powerless in today's world?* Do we welcome people only on *our* terms? Do we expect certain things of visitors who come our way? Do we expect them to look and act in a certain way before we're truly willing to welcome them? Does it seem that there is a growing rift between traditional Sunday School classes and a secular world? Is there a desire present to heal that rift?

4. *Is change even possible? At what price? And are we willing to pay that price? Is there a way to be Christ-like and comfortable at the same time?*

These are a few of the questions that will be dealt with in Chapters 1 and 2. Particularly as you read Chapter 2, be aware that the experience may not be entirely comfortable. My desire is that you approach the issues to be raised there as prayerfully and honestly as possible.

# Chapter 1:
## Sunday School 101

The Sunday School is the best known institution of Christian education among evangelicals today. It is so much a part of Christian education that it seems almost normative. Many presume it has always existed, but such is not the case. In fact, the Sunday School is relatively new.[1]

### *Sunday School beginnings*

The roots of the Sunday School movement may be traced to **Robert Raikes** (1735-1811), a wealthy newspaperman and philanthropist, in Gloucester, England. Raikes was a champion of the poor and a frequent visitor to local prisons, becoming involved in teaching prisoners to read and write. Of particular concern to him were the children of the poor classes he saw running about on Sundays. However, under the Enabling Act of 1779, he was legally barred from establishing a school with any person or group outside the Church of England. These were children of the factories and could hardly have attended anyway.[2]

*Are there children in your community who do not attend Sunday School because of their socio-economic or cultural setting? What is your church's responsibility for those children?*

Raikes met this challenge in 1780 by renting a building and conducting a Sunday school for these children. Teachers were paid a modest stipend to provide secular and religious instruction. The objective of the school was to teach literacy; the primary textbook was the Bible. Classes began at 10:00 AM, broke for lunch at noon, and resumed in the afternoon with catechetical instruction and worship until 5:00 PM.[3] Each child would stand for inspection before being admitted, a washed face being the price of entry. As they piled out the door, each child would be given a coin for having attended. Finances eventually came to be a problem. Raikes, the newspaperman, published an account of his school to be read widely, even beyond Great Britain. A result of this publicity was the establishment of the Sunday School Society in 1785. Payment of teachers continued to drain the resources until John Wesley identified himself with the movement, calling for volunteer teachers to replace paid ones.[4]

> *Why do you believe the Sunday School was initially opposed by the church? Why do some churches today tend to oppose para-church religious movements?*

Robert Raikes and his children, otherwise known as "Bobby Wild-Goose and his ragged regiment" were controversial to say the least. The Church of England opposed the movement, its clergy deeming it a desecration of the Sabbath. John Wesley was among the first clergymen to endorse the movement. His support greatly aided the acceptance of the Sunday School by the church. The first known Baptist to be associated with the Sunday School was William Fox, a wealthy layman and contemporary of Raikes. It was Fox who assisted in the formation of the Sunday School Society. The movement continued to grow. Conservative estimates put the enrollment of Sunday schools at 400,000 at the time of Raikes' death in 1811, and 1,250,000 by 1831. The Sunday School Union was formed in 1803 and gradually replaced the Society. The Union started a Sunday school teacher's manual in 1813.[5]

A parallel movement started in the United States. Reed and Provost place the date of Sunday schools in America well before 1780. These schools came about for different reasons than those in England. Most of those who come to this country did so with deep religious convictions that naturally included a desire for the religious training of their children.

> John Wesley may have begun something akin to a Sunday School in Savannah, Georgia, in 1737. Similar institutions sprang up in Ephrata, Pennsylvania, in 1739; in Bethlehem, Connecticut, in 1740; and in Philadelphia, Pennsylvania, in 1744. The purpose of these schools was explicitly and implicitly religious and denominational. They were linked directly to and sponsored by churches.[6]

These schools died out due to lack of support by churches. They did, however, pave the way for the permanent establishment of Sunday Schools in this country.

**William Elliott** is generally thought to be the pioneer of the Sunday School movement in the United States. His school started out much like that of Raikes, focusing attention on the poor. He opened his home on Sunday evenings to teach his own children, the children of his slaves, and any neighbor child who might drop by. Others followed this example. By 1790, the Sabbath School Society was established in Philadelphia.[7] As in England, the movement grew quickly in this country. The American Sunday School Union was established in 1824. Through the influence of this group, Sunday Schools were part of the westward movement and at times sufficed for public education. By 1832, 8,268 Sunday Schools in 27 states and the District of Columbia were affiliated with the American

Sunday School Union. By 1875, this number had grown to 65,000.[8] In 1889, it was claimed that at least 10 million people were enrolled in American Sunday Schools. If this is true, the figure would have represented one-sixth the population of this country.[9]

Even before the establishment of the Southern Baptist Convention in 1845, Sunday Schools had already become part of Baptist churches throughout the South. Their curriculum materials came from a variety of sources, including the Triennial Convention. In 1872, the Uniform Lesson Committee was established to provide lesson outlines for Sunday Schools. Southern Baptists were well represented on that committee and continued to utilize its outlines to at least some degree throughout the twentieth century.

## *Lessons from our history*

When the Southern Baptist Convention was formed, two missions agencies came into existence: the Foreign Mission Board, located in Richmond, Virginia, and the Board of Domestic Missions in Augusta, Georgia.[10] In 1891, after several failed attempts, the Baptist Sunday School Board was organized in Nashville, Tennessee, by Dr. J.M. Frost. This agency, presently known as LifeWay Christian Resources of the Southern Baptist Convention, is the largest publisher of religious materials in the world. It was the first privately-owned business to have its own postal zip code (37234), and is reportedly the largest private user of the United States Postal Service. The "Sunday School Board," as it still known by many, has included many departments of work through the years in addition to Sunday School. These include Discipleship Training (known by a variety of names), Church Music, Church Administration, and Church Architecture. LifeWay is much more than a publisher of Sunday School curriculum materials. The agency is home to four publishers: Broadman & Holman (trade and academic books), Holman Bible Publishers, Genevox (church music), and LifeWay Press (denominationally-oriented books). LifeWay also operates numerous book stores throughout the country and owns two national conference centers, Glorieta and Ridgecrest. Some of this diversity began in 1920 with the establishment of the Sunday School department. Below is a brief summary of the leaders of the Sunday School department, beginning with its first Secretary, Mr. Arthur Flake.

**Flake's Formula**
1. Know the possibilities
2. Enlarge the organization
3. Provide the space
4. Enlist and train the workers
5. Go after the people

***The Arthur Flake Period, Years of Learning, 1920-1943.***-- By 1920, the Southern Baptist Convention was publishing materials for all ages through its Board in Nashville. Arthur Flake, a hardware store owner in

Winona, Mississippi, was the man who taught Southern Baptists how to grow Sunday Schools. Mr. Flake's business was successful, primarily because he planned and took necessary steps for growth. He researched his customer base, determined their needs, organized his store around those needs, trained a corps of salesmen, enlarged his store as needed, and launched an advertising campaign. Mr. Flake was also Sunday School superintendent at the local Baptist church and began applying these same growth principles to the Bible teaching organization. These principles soon proved applicable in a church setting as evidenced by the rapid growth of his Sunday School. In 1909, he went to work as a field consultant for the Baptist Sunday School Board. He was the leader of Southern Baptist Sunday Schools from 1920 to 1943.[11] The principles which he taught became known as Flake's Formula.[12]

***The J.N. Barnette period, Years of Growing, 1943-1957.--*** J. N. Barnette, an assistant and later a successor to Flake, developed through observation and personal experience a set of laws by which Sunday School could grow most effectively. (See Figure 1). These laws are still applicable today.

# Figure 1
# J. N. Barnette's Laws[13]

| The law related to... | The law, briefly stated |
|---|---|
| Number of Workers | Enrollment in Sunday School increases in proportion to the number of workers at the ratio of 10:1. |
| Size of Units | Units (classes) normally reach their maximum growth within a few months after they are started. |
| New Units | New units grow faster and win more people to Christ and provide more workers than older units. |
| Grading | Grading by ages provides the logical basis for adding new units. |
| Promotion | Promotion on the basis of age follows the natural laws of growth and development. Annual promotion is necessary. |
| Visitation | Enrollment and attendance increase in proportion to the number of visits made. |
| The Building | The building sets the pattern for Sunday School growth. A Sunday School cannot successfully grow beyond the capacity of its building.[14] |

Perhaps Barnette is equally to be remembered for leading Southern Baptist Sunday Schools through years of unprecedented growth. During the period in which he was Secretary (Director) of the Sunday School Department, enrollment more than doubled, from 3,188,341 to 6,827,713.[15] The greatest year of growth under his leadership was 1954. The "Million More in 54" campaign that swept through Southern Baptist churches was almost successful. That year, nearly 850,000 were added to Baptist Sunday School rolls. Education ministry as a profession came into its own during the post-war years of Barnette's tenure as lay leadership found it increasingly difficult to keep pace with the unprecedented growth.

**The A. V. Washburn Period, Years of Developing, 1957-1978.--** A.V. Washburn was first to use the title of *Director* of the Sunday School Department. The change in job title was symbolic of many changes which transpired during this period. One was a move, along with other Southern Baptist program organizations, to the *Grouping-Grading* plan. For the first time, all denominational agencies would follow the same pattern, pioneered by the Brotherhood Commission in the introduction of its new materials in 1960. School age grading was now the pattern through the twelfth grade, and the seven age divisions were reduced to four.

> ***The old age groupings***
> Nursery, birth - age 3
> Beginner, ages 4-5
> Primary, ages 6-8
> Junior, ages 9-12
> Intermediate, ages 13-16
> Young People, ages 17-24
> Adult, 25 and up

> ***The new age groupings***
> Preschool - birth - pre-first grade
> Children - Grades 1-6
> Youth - Grades 7-12
> Adult - 18 (or marriage) and up

The other major change during this era was the introduction of the new *Life and Work* curriculum series in 1966. Prior to this time, all Southern Baptists had been using the Uniform lessons (renamed "Convention Uniform" in 1966). *Convention Uniform* was a series of topical studies using the King James version and was based on lesson outlines developed by the interdenominational Uniform Lesson Committee. The *Life and Work* series was distinctively Southern Baptist and was available to all four age divisions. Its lesson outlines were developed by editors at the Baptist Sunday School Board and grew out of the perceived needs of learners at every age. It was the more "age-graded" of the two series, providing separate materials for eleven age groupings rather than the four of the Convention Uniform series.

During the Washburn era, the influence of Arthur Flake was not felt as keenly as before. New concepts in reaching people were developed, and the concept of open Sunday School enrollment was endorsed. This was the view that persons could be enrolled in Sunday School any time and any place, as long as they gave their permission. The open enrollment concept is still the official Sunday School enrollment strategy.

***The Harry Piland Period, Years of Renewing, 1978-1994.--*** Harry Piland[16] came to this position as one of the most loved and respected ministers of education in Southern Baptist life, having served in several large and influential churches, including Hyde Park in Austin and First Baptist, Houston. When Piland assumed leadership of the Bible Teaching Division, as it was called by then, Sunday School enrollment growth had slowed to a virtual standstill across the Southern Baptist Convention. He launched the *8.5 by 85* campaign with the goal of raising Sunday School enrolment by more than a million by 1985. While not entirely successful, Southern Baptist Sunday Schools topped the 8 million mark for the first time. A new curriculum series, *Bible Book*, was added in 1980. It was later renamed *Explore the Bible*. This latest choice gave Sunday School teachers of youth and adults the option of a content-oriented series featuring a systematic study of the books of the Bible in a nine-year rotation.[17]

### Nine Basics of Sunday School Growth
1. Make a commitment to growth
2. Identify and enroll prospects
3. Start new classes and departments
4. Enlist workers
5. Train workers
6. Provide space and equipment
7. Conduct weekly workers' meetings
8. Conduct weekly visitation
9. Teach the Bible to win the lost and develop the saved

Piland returned to some of the more basic values of earlier years, recasting "Flake's Formula" into his "Nine Basics."[18]

## Lessons from the present

***The Bill Taylor Period, Years of \_\_\_\_-?, 1994-2001.--*** The question mark above does not stem from any sense of pessimism concerning this most recent administration of Sunday School work. History has not yet had the opportunity to assess the leadership of this period.

If I were to insert a word into that blank at this time, this era would be defined as *Years of Reinventing*. The Taylor years have been characterized by constant change, or as many would prefer to say, constant improvement. These changes have included curriculum materials, the philosophy of the Sunday School, the name of the agency itself, and of course, the organization (and reorganization) of the staff of the Sunday School division. Concerning the latter, a popular joke among staff members of the Sunday School department goes like this: As an editor leaves his office to go to lunch he gives this message to his secretary: "If my boss calls, find out who it is."[19]

One of the most noticeable changes has been in the agency's name. In 1998, the name of the Baptist Sunday School Board was officially changed to LifeWay Christian Resources of the Southern Baptist Convention. This gave the Bible Teaching and Reaching Division an opportunity to request and be granted the privilege of changing its name back to the Sunday School Division.

The great challenge that Bill Taylor and others in the Sunday School Division have faced has been that of preparing Sunday School to make the transition to the 21st century. To make that transition, it was agreed that Sunday School needed to be viewed less as a traditional church program organization with its own program objectives to be carried out and more of a strategy to reach a greater end. The resulting definition appears in the box to the right.[20]

> *Sunday School is the foundational strategy for leading people to faith in the Lord Jesus and for building Great Commission Christians through Bible study groups that engage people in evangelism, discipleship, fellowship, ministry, and worship.*

Earlier in Taylor's administration of the Sunday School division, the Sunday School year in churches was redefined. Prior to that change, the "quarters" were October-December, January-March, and so forth. Starting in September, 1998, the quarters were aligned with the seasons of the year, and September became the beginning of the Sunday School year. For most churches, the annual promotion day and beginning of the Sunday School year could now coincide with the beginning of public school.

In Fall, 2000, new curriculum changes were introduced. The *Family Bible Series* (formerly *Convention Uniform series*) was eliminated. The *Life and Work* series disappeared, and in its place came the new *Family Bible Study* series, not to be confused with the older series with a similar name. Only the *Explore the Bible* series was continued, though in a redesigned format. The four age divisions were adjusted to become five.

> **Current Age Divisions**
> Preschool: Birth-Kindergarten
> Children: Grades 1-6
> Youth: Grades 7-12
> Young Adult: 18-24
> Adult: 25 and above

The real emphasis of these changes has been on the Family Bible Study materials which blended together some of the features of both the series it replaced. The result was a fully age-graded series that allowed every member of the family to study the same basic passage. This writer was one of the first to contribute lessons to the new series. The organizing principle for the reinvented Sunday School was the "1-5-4

Principle of Growth," developed by LifeWay Church Resources President Gene Mims:[21]

Rather than revise the program purpose statements of Sunday School, the new leadership team has chosen to express Sunday School's mission in terms of the following strategic principles.[22]

➡ **The Principle of Foundational Evangelism:**
Sunday School is the most basic evangelism strategy of the church. Evangelism is rooted in on-going, open Bible study groups that provide a safe haven for new believers and a place where they can be nurtured. Its organizational structure provides an ideal network for sharing information concerning lost people as well as the mobilization of members to reach out to the lost. It serves to promote short-term Bible study and evangelism training events which can equip members to be involved in reaching the lost. Sunday School also provides for preschoolers and children a foundation for evangelism by teaching basic truths concerning God and His love, Jesus and His life on earth, and the helpers (disciples) who told others the good news of Jesus.

> **1** *driving force for church growth:*
> **The Great Commission**
>
> **5** *essential church functions for church growth:*
> **Evangelism • Discipleship • Fellowship • Ministry • Worship**
>
> **4** *results:*
> **Numerical Growth • Spiritual Growth • Ministries Expansion • Missions Advance**

➡ **The Principle of Foundational Discipleship:**
Sunday School is the beginning point for discipleship. Through Bible study and the encouragement for families to study the Bible together, Sunday School undergirds these basic functions of the church: evangelism, discipleship, ministry, fellowship, and worship. It provides help to believers of all ages by providing a balanced curriculum intended to help them mature as disciples who are equipped to carry out the Great Commission. At the same time, Sunday School points to other more intensive study opportunities. Through training in discipleship, Sunday School promotes the involvement of all believers in a personal ministry. It encourages Christian stewardship of life and possessions. It encourages participation in the church's overall mission in the community and the world.

➥ **The Principle of Family Responsibility:**
The Sunday School teaches parents to fulfill their role as the primary religious educators of their children and provides encouragement for them as they exemplify the Christian life to their children. It seeks to nurture sound and healthy families through balanced Bible study and through pointing to special studies designed around the needs of both healthy and hurting families. It teaches Christian parents to be evangelists in their own home, and it seeks to win to Christ the unsaved parents of children who attend.

➥ **The Principle of Spiritual Transformation:**
The Sunday School understands and teaches that it is the destiny of every believer to become *conformed to the likeness of Christ.* It teaches a life of obedience. It helps Christians through the struggles that ensue when the biblical world view challenges the secular world view in which they still may be engaged. It promotes a transformation both of belief and behavior. It helps Christians of all ages to deal with common life issues. It encourages and equips Christians to serve on the spiritual front lines of their communities, homes, schools, and work places.

➥ **The Principle of Biblical Leadership**
Sunday School recognizes the pastor as the primary leader of the church as it seeks to build Great Commission Christians. At the same time, it recognizes the leadership potential within believers throughout the congregation and helps to develop that potential. Sunday School provides opportunities for emerging leaders to serve through outreach, evangelism, teaching, ministry, and missions. It helps them to discover and develop their spiritual gifts. It points growing Christians to more intensive opportunities of leadership development. Its own teachers and leaders exemplify these principles as they not only "teach the lesson" but "become the lesson" as well.

**10 Best Practices**
1. Commit to the Strategy
2. Organize with a Purpose
3. Build Kingdom Leaders
4. Develop Soul Winners
5. Win the Lost
6. Assimilate People
7. Partner with Families
8. Teach to Transform
9. Mobilize for Ministry
10. Multiply Leaders and Units

In 2001, Bill Taylor and Ken Hemphill introduced the book, *Ten Best Practices to Make Your Sunday School Work.* The ten practices are listed briefly to the right, and are expressions of the strategic principles listed above.[23]

*The _____ Period, 2001–and beyond: Toward an Uncharted Future.–* Between April and October of 2001, some of the most sweeping changes imaginable were instituted at LifeWay Church Resources.[24] At the time of this writing, the dust has not yet settled on just what some of these changes will be. In the light of the history of Southern Baptist Sunday School reviewed on these pages, one change stands out: There is for the first time no *Director* of the Sunday School Department (or Division) at the national level. The staff at LifeWay Church Resources will be organized quite differently. Bill Taylor has been named Director of Networking Partnerships. His team will network with other denominational agencies, state conventions, and educational institutions. There will now be no separation between the programs organizations such as Sunday School and Discipleship Training. The Discipleship Training Department will no longer exist. Editorial and production staff will form age-group teams to develop and edit all products related to that age division including open Bible study groups, discipleship, and Vacation Bible School. A team of field service representatives will be stationed throughout the United States; these will be under the leadership of the age-level teams.

Because of the sweeping nature of these changes, an unusual and to some a controversial administrative decision was announced in April, 2001: All positions within the LifeWay Church Resources division would cease to exist as of October 1, 2001.[25] Employees would have the option of re-applying and interviewing for a position within the new organization. On their application, they could state a preference for up to three positions. Those who did not reapply or who were not rehired would cease to be employed as of October 1, 2001. Representatives of LifeWay indicated that almost all affected employees did reapply and were rehired, generally to one of the positions for which they had indicated a preference.

Once the difficulties have been ironed out, this new organization has the potential of achieving better coordination between product lines and of virtually eliminating competition among those lines. At the same time, LifeWay Church Resources should now be more accessible to the average Southern Baptist pastor through the availability of a LifeWay consultant in his area.[26]

## *What have we learned?*

What conclusions may be drawn from these lessons? First, let me suggest that *the principles and laws of growth developed by Flake and Barnette still work.* Countless pastors and ministers of education, including this writer, have proven this over and over. In my own ministry, Sunday School growth was achieved every time the principles were implemented. In fact, that growth was in proportion to my commitment to the principles. During the years in which Southern Baptists departed from these operating principles, the growth of Sunday Schools came to a virtual halt. The growth of Sunday School within the denomination resumed when Dr. Piland began reimplementing these basic principles.

Second, *it is more helpful to think of Sunday School as a strategy rather than as a program.* As a program, Sunday School has fixed purposes. Our purpose then becomes that of helping Sunday School to achieve its purposes. Until the Taylor era, these stated purposes had been to

1. Reach persons for Bible study
2. Teach the Bible
3. Witness to persons about Christ and lead them into church membership
4. Minister to persons in need
5. Lead members to worship
6. Interpret and undergird the work of the church and the denomination.[27]

For many years it seems that our chief purpose in educational work has been to build strong Sunday Schools, but we could never seem to figure out why. Some suggested that it was so that another generation of Sunday School teachers and church leaders could be produced so that future Sunday Schools might be strong. But what would be the purpose of *those* Sunday Schools? You get the idea. By expressing Sunday School as strategy, it is possible to focus on an ultimate objective: *Preparing God's people to serve on the front lines.* Certainly, the front lines begin at home as believers are equipped to pass the heritage of faith on to new generations. The front lines extend to the community, the workplace, and the world. Much of this book will focus on these front lines. The foundational principles developed by Taylor and Hanks provide helpful ways of exploring Sunday School as a transformational strategy. To the five they have listed, however, I would like to suggest two others:

> **Sunday School exists to prepare God's people for service on the front lines.**

➥ **The Principle of Christlike Ministry**
Sunday School is a basic strategy for ministry to members and non-members. Organizationally, it creates a ministry network that not only touches the lives of each member and guest but can also impact the lives of the lost and unchurched throughout the community. Functionally, it promotes the personal ministry of each believer. Sunday School teaches believers to be like Jesus and to embody His presence in a lost world. It teaches members to understand and employ the ministry style of Jesus: being loving, accepting,

non-judgmental, inclusive, non-traditional, non-prejudicial, healing, and always redemptive.

➡ **The Principle of Global Awareness**
Missions was initially at the very heart of the Sunday School, and in the 21$^{st}$ century, it is beginning to be once more. Sunday School teaches a biblical basis for missions. It teaches that us that ours is a God who still sends His people out. Sunday School provides information concerning the national and global missions enterprises of Southern Baptists and a means of networking with missionaries. It encourages prayer and financial support for missions. It instills within the heart of believers the missionary message and mandate. Sunday School teaches believers to "Think Globally, but Act Locally."

Finally, let me suggest that *to make Sunday School truly effective as a strategy, we must stop magnifying its traditions and begin focusing on its potential.* Through the pages of this book, you'll see many ways that we have "institutionalized" Sunday School and its traditions. In doing so, we have robbed it of its greatest strength: helping believers to experience the transforming power of God's Word.

*Notes*

# *Endnotes*

1. James E. Reed and Ronnie Provost, *A History of Christian Education.* (Nashville: Broadman & Holman, 1993) p. 255.

2. Ibid, pp. 256-257.

3. Ibid, p. 258.

4. Charles A. Tidwell, *The Educational Ministry of the Church,* Revised Edition. (Nashville: Broadman & Holman, 1996), p. 33.

5. Reed and Provost, pp. 258-260.

6. Ibid, p. 260.

7. C. B. Eavey, *History of Christian Education.* (Chicago: Moody Press, 1964), pp. 231-232.

8. Anne M. Boylan, *Sunday School: The Formation of an American Institution*, 2nd ed. (New Haven, Connecticut: Yale University Press, 1988), pp. 31-33, in Reed and Provost, pp. 262-263.

9. Gerald E. Knoff, *The World Sunday School Movement: The Story of a Broadening Mission* (New York: Seabury Press, 1979), p. 3, in Reed and Provost, p. 263.

10. Later, the Board of Domestic Missions was renamed the Home Mission Board and moved to Atlanta, Georgia. In 1997, these two agencies were renamed the International Mission Board, still located in Richmond, and the North American Mission Board in Alpharetta, Georgia.

11. Ibid, p. 21.

12. Charles A. Tidwell, *Educational Ministry of a Church.* (Nashville: Broadman Press, 1982), p. 249.

13. Ibid., pp. 249-250.

14. Generally, this law still holds true. Recent trends toward multiple use of buildings such as dual Sunday School, and non-traditional places for Bible study classes have tended to modify this law in some instances.

15. Piland, p. 24.

16. Dr. Piland passed away on May 24, 2001, after a lengthy illness.

17. Several years later, *Explore the Bible for Youth* was readjusted to a six-year cycle, more in keeping with the years youth spent in that division.

18. Ibid., p. 251.

19. Effective September 2001, Bill Taylor's position was changed to reflect responsibility over Sunday School field service personnel. At the time of this writing, it appears that Bill Taylor will not be replaced as Sunday School Director. The chief administrator of Sunday School and the other program organizations will very likely be Gene Mims, President of LifeWay Church Resources.

20. Bill Taylor and Louis Hanks, *Sunday School for a New Century.* (Nashville: LifeWay Press, 1999), p. 11.

21. Gene Mims, *Kingdom Principles for Church Growth.* (Nashville: Convention Press, 1994), p. 4.

22. The foundational principles are quotations from Taylor and Hanks, pp. 20-21. The descriptions are my own summaries and interpretations of their material.

23. Ken Hemphill and Bill Taylor, *Ten Best Practices to Make Your Sunday School Work.* (Nashville: LifeWay Press, 2001), p. 3.

24. A reminder: LifeWay Church Resources is a division of LifeWay Christian Resources. The division is headed by Gene Mims, its president, and includes all materials, resources, and strategies that impact churches and their programming. Included in this division are personnel who relate to such materials as Sunday School, Discipleship Training, Family Ministry, and Vacation Bible School.

25. This policy affected approximately 700 employees at every level with the exception of the top administration. This number represents approximately half of the employees of LifeWay Christian Resources.

26. LifeWay consultants, as of this writing, will be assigned to serve an area of approximately 1000 churches. Oklahoma, with approximately 1700 churches, will probably have two consultants. These consultants will represent every age division and every product available through LifeWay Church Resources.

27. Harry M. Piland and Ernest Adams, *BreakThrough: Sunday School Work.* (Nashville: Convention Press, 1990), p. 10.

# Chapter 2:
## Counting the Cost

The new minister of education was presiding over his first teachers' meeting. New beginnings are generally exciting, but the honeymoon in this church was short-lived. An adult worker stood up. "Bro. Bob," she began, "I think I speak for all of us when I say, 'You leave us alone and we'll leave you alone.'"

The eight-year veteran of educational ministry wasn't used to "leaving his workers alone." At the same time, he understood what the woman meant. The Sunday School in that church had not grown for many years. The adult division consisted of a dozen or so classes, most of which had been organized for more than fifty years. Each of the classes could have shared the same story: Since their separate beginnings, they had maintained their original membership. No one had promoted in, and certainly no one had promoted out. Each class had its roster of officers, its own class business meetings, and its own traditions. One class even kept its classroom locked and maintained strict control of the keys. Cleaning was done by appointment with the church custodian under the watchful eye of a class officer. None of the classes had shown any interest in growing by including new people.

Other ministers of education had attempted to reorganize these classes and had failed. The new man would probably be no different. Actually, he could have expected this response to his opening "pep talk." He had done his homework. The old, traditional church had at one time been one of the largest in the city. For the past ten years, there had been steady decline from an average attendance of more than 1,400 each week to fewer than 400. The old church seemed to be dying. The new religious educator thought he had some answers, but no one wanted to hear them.

> *Why did this church apparently not want to grow? Why did it seem to be dying – in the midst of a large city?*

## *Facing our failures*

> *...and every day, the Lord added those being saved to them. Believers in the Lord in increasing numbers – crowds of both men and women And look, you have filled Jerusalem with your teaching...* Acts 2:47, 5:14, and 5:28, HCSB.[1]

*Page 17*

It is impossible to read the book of Acts without seeing church growth on practically every page. From some 120 witnesses of Christ's ascension, the church grew to 3,000 on the day of Pentecost. By the time of Peter's second sermon, that number had grown to 5,000. The early believers in Jerusalem were well regarded by their neighbors. The church grew through daily witnessing efforts at the Temple and in homes throughout Jerusalem. Soon, the message of Jesus had penetrated the entire city.

Jerusalem could not contain that wonderful message. The Gospel soon spread in all directions. Philip, a deacon, took the good news to the hated Samaritans. An Ethiopian official took the message back to his home and the Gospel took root in North Africa. Even the obstinate Peter shared it with Cornelius, a Gentile. At first, the message was spread through intentional acts of obedience by early believers. The tactic of the religious establishment was to persecute these believers through arrests, beatings, and even stonings. Persecution served only to spread the message, not extinguish it.

Judaism could not even contain this message. It was, after all, for all mankind. The Gentiles were receptive and responded quickly. There came a time when everyone in Asia Minor – Jew and Gentile alike – had the opportunity to hear the story of Jesus. All of this happened quickly. From Jerusalem to Rome and in almost every town in between, the gospel took root. The remarkable events described in the book of Acts took place over a period of some thirty years.

We have the same gospel the early believers had. We even have advantages they didn't have: A full New Testament, the witness of 2000 years of Christian history, and unprecedented means of mass communication and rapid travel. *Why, then, hasn't the gospel penetrated our cities and towns? Why are more churches today declining than growing? Why are Christians a smaller proportion of society than forty years ago?*

*What about your church? Is it making an impact on the surrounding community? Are the lives of people being changed through the ministries of your church and its Sunday School?*

There are a number of possibilities to consider. Some blame the rising secularism in our society. But is rising secularism a cause or an effect of an ineffective church? Some suggest increased competition for time, with activities that pull families in many different directions. Perhaps an African-American pastor in a nearby city came close to the truth in a discussion with a small group of Anglo pastors. The group was lamenting the fact that neither their churches nor their Sunday

Schools were growing. Several pastors gave excuses for the lack of growth, and others suggested possible reasons. The Black pastor said, "Brothers, I think I know why. It's because your White churches *try to keep the outside out and the inside in.*" It is the thesis of this chapter that many of our churches are not growing because they simply do not wish to pay the price to grow. Let's examine the cost to be paid first by members, then by staff.

## *The cost to be paid by members*

**1 The cost of relinquishing ownership**
Whose church is this, anyway? Most long-time members could make a pretty good case for claiming ownership of the church. After all, many have sacrificed to pay the bills. Countless volunteer hours have been spent in building, repairing, and keeping up the property. I even know one church whose older members had grown up in homes where their houses had been mortgaged by their parents to pay for their building constructed during the Depression. The fact that members have served faithfully through the years, have seen pastors come and go, and have been there through thick and thin should give them a legitimate claim to ownership of the church. Shouldn't it? Not when we consider what Christ did for the church. He established the Church. He died to redeem it. He empowered it with His Spirit and instructed it with His Word. One day, Christ will return to claim it for Himself. Jesus said, *I will build my church* (from Matthew 16:18). Christ is indeed the owner of the church, and that includes its Sunday School classes.

Gary, a friend and pastor of a small church in Seattle, Washington, told me this story: Although his church was in the midst of a vast mission field, it simply was not growing. Gary prayed, he preached, he taught, and he led, all with one focus: to somehow inspire his people to love the lost and seek to win them. Nothing happened. He finally confided in a friend of his, a Canadian pastor named Henry Blackaby. Dr. Blackaby reminded him of Jesus' claim to ownership of the church in Matthew 16:18 and of His promise to build it. Gary was advised to lead his church to return itself to its rightful Owner.

Over the next few weeks, that became his mission and the focus of his teaching and preaching efforts. Members understood and accepted the necessity of following that advice. The result was an evening service when the members did indeed surrender their claim to ownership of the church. At the end of the service, a stranger came in and asked to speak with the pastor. While the members were still around, Pastor Gary announced, "Folks, you'll want to hear this." The congregation was seated and the stranger began speaking in broken English. He introduced himself as a former pastor of a Baptist church in Lugansk, Ukraine. "God sent me to your church to give you this," he continued, and pulled an envelope out of his coat pocket and handed it to the pastor. Gary opened the document written in Russian. "This is a deed to my house in Lugansk. I'm giving the house to your church."

> *Are there some "ownership issues" in your church? If so, how might they be overcome?*

"We can't possibly accept....." Gary began, then stopped. He wanted to say that the church couldn't accept the house because there would be nothing they could do with it. He couldn't imagine his little church owning property in the Soviet Union. Then he said to his congregation, "I can't finish that sentence. Because of what we've just done, I do not have the right to, and neither do you. Let's ask the Owner what He wants to do with this house." The end result of this story was that the 50-member church with less than $100 in the bank was able to direct a missions ministry in Lugansk, a city of a million people. Through that ministry, literally thousands of people in the Ukraine have come to know Christ as Savior.[2]

## 2 The cost of surrendering prejudices

Surrendered ownership of one's church or Sunday School class may mean surrendering something else: prejudice. We accept some people; we reject others. Sometimes this is on the basis of race. I have an African American friend who attended a funeral a few years ago in a predominantly white church. She was well-dressed and well-educated, and she was in the company of a number of Anglo friends from her work place. The group came in and sat down on a pew where there were people already sitting. A distinguished woman looked at my friend in utter disgust, and got up and moved.

Let me make a confession. I was the minister of education in the opening illustration in this chapter. One of the traditional women's classes in that church had its own membership committee. New members were admitted only after a screening interview by and a recommendation from the membership committee.

The problem of prejudice can cut across all age groups. A teenage musician I knew was pretty good and had quite a following among the "street kids" of his town. He told me of the experience of bringing one of his unchurched friends to his Sunday School. The guest was an atheist who agreed to go out of curiosity. He wore the usual array of earrings and nose rings, and his hair was of a color not found in nature. His clothes were even worse. Tragically, the young atheist was shunned by the Christian teenagers and their leaders alike. He never returned.

The cost of surrendering prejudices is that our people must be willing to love all the people Jesus loved and to share Christ's love and their friendship with them. Many apparently feel that the cost is too great. Read the following chart and draw your own conclusions.

## Figure 2[3]

| Ministry Comparison Chart ||
|---|---|
| **Ministry Characteristics of Jesus** | **Ministry Characteristics of Scribes and Pharisees** |
| Accepted everyone – even the poor, lame, blind, lepers, sinners | Accepted only people like themselves: the wealthy and influential |
| He was criticized by the religious establishment | They were the religious establishment of their day |
| Broke with tradition whenever necessary | Were slaves to tradition |
| Met people where they were to teach, reach, heal | Confined their teaching to the Temple and synagogues |
| Interested in what was in their hearts | Interested in the outward appearance of people |
| Lived what He taught | Taught one thing and lived another |
| Practiced God's law of love | Amended God's law with man-made rules |
| *Which list contains more characteristics of your church or Sunday School class?* ||

**3 The cost of being relevant**
Dr. Thom Rainer, in his book, *The Bridger Generation*, identified four generations of Americans and indicated the percentage of that generation that professed to be Christian. (Refer to Figure 3). It is very likely that our Sunday School classes and the traditions behind them are much more relevant to the two older generations than to the younger ones. Consider the following check list:

- ☐ Does your Sunday School offer non-traditional times and places for Bible study in addition to the traditional Sunday morning classes?

- ☐ Is the racial and sociological diversity that exists in your community reflected in those who attend your Sunday School classes? Your worship services?

- ☐ Is your Sunday School well attended by persons in your immediate community (as opposed to the vast majority driving a considerable distance to your church)?

- ☐ Is the growth rate of your Sunday School keeping pace with the growth of your community or your city?

- ☐ Does the membership of individual classes change from year to year because of annual promotion or reorganization (as opposed to staying the same)?

- ☐ Does your church provide a curriculum based on the needs of individual groups (as opposed to using a "standard" curriculum)?

- ☐ Does your church provide classes for persons with special needs such as Sunday workers, handicapped, or mentally retarded?

In many of our churches and Sunday School classes, ministry decisions are made on the basis of what *members want*. Perhaps we should begin making decisions based on what *lost people need*. What would change if by this time next year you could check all the boxes above? Would your members be willing to pay the price?

### Figure 3[4]
### Generations of Americans

| Generation | Birth Years | Percentage Reached for Christ |
|---|---|---|
| Builders | Before 1946 | **65%** |
| Boomers | 1946-1964 | **35%** |
| Busters | 1965-1976 | **15%** |
| Bridgers | 1977-1994 | **4%** |

## 4 The cost of shifting identity

Your Sunday School classes and your congregation have personalities. You may be known as a "blue collar" church, a "yuppie" church, or a family-oriented community church. Your church's identity emerges from the individual identities of many of its members. As a result, some people presently on the outside will feel comfortable with you while others will not.

> *What groups of people in your community would have a hard time identifying with the members of your congregation?*

How would an influx of new members affect your church or Sunday School? A church in Oklahoma attempted to start a satellite ministry. It purchased a church facility in another neighborhood where a small core of members from the original church were attending. In many ways, the satellite was ideally located. It was situated in the middle of several of the fastest growing communities in the city. The pastor advised those families attending the church's main campus to remain where they were. He felt that the space was needed for the new families who lived near the satellite. There was a problem, however. Because of the failure of the satellite members to change their identity, the new people were simply not reached. The satellite failed and the property was sold to another church. Receiving new members from the community can often mean a shift in the basic identity of your congregation or of your Sunday School classes. If this happened, would members be willing to pay the price?

## 5 The cost of changing personal relationships

Most Baptists enjoy their Sunday School classes. They're comfortable, and that's where they might expect to find their friends. This, in fact, is the basis of a very real problem. Most people need a certain number of friends in their lives. If those friendships are found in their Sunday School classes, everyone tends to be happy. Many of our classes consist of people whose need for friends are being met by other members of the class.

How does this impact the new people who come your way? Imagine that a Christian who has just moved to your city visits your class. He has left his old friends behind and is in need of new ones. If he comes to your class, will he find people who are eager to reach out to him and include him? Or will he find people whose needs for friendships are being met, and who don't particularly need any new ones? The same is true of new Christians. Many will have just left behind their old circle of friends. They will be desperate for new ones.

Many have observed a disturbing trend: Half of the people who join a Baptist church or a Sunday School class will become inactive within six months. Why? Probably not because of the quality of teaching or preaching. To the contrary, these may have been the things that drew them in initially. The problem for most is they have failed to establish new relationships. Some classes remain constant year after year, failing to promote members in and out. Many teachers have a possessive attitude toward their members, not wanting to lose anyone to other classes, even as teachers. These were the problems of the old church mentioned in the opening illustration in this chapter. The solution involves age-grading, annual promotion, and periodic reorganization due to growth. There is a price to be paid for this, in terms of the willingness to accept changing personal relationships. Are your members willing to pay this price?

## 6 The cost of accepting responsibility

It's a bit ironic, but the same individual who feels that the church belongs to him when decisions need to be made suddenly feels that it's someone else's church when it comes time to serve. One of the great tragedies of major denominations today is that they have made the "ministry" into a profession. The term "minister" in many churches is a masculine term and refers to the pastor and other "ministerial" staff members. If Paul is correct in Ephesians 4:11-12, the term "minister" is actually gender-neutral and belongs to all of God's people!

Rank-and-file members need to be taught that from day one they are ministers of the Gospel of Jesus Christ. Remember the old church that had declined from 1400 to 400 in average attendance? I was speaking with a deacon in that church one day. Believing he was my "boss," he proceeded to tell me several things I needed to be doing. I asked him to run his suggestions by one of my two bosses. When asked to explain, I replied that other than the Lord, I had two bosses in that church: my pastor, and my congregation acting as a body. If either of my bosses approved his plan, I would be happy to comply. When the conversation was redirected to ways in which he could be serving, he informed me that it was his job to pay the bills. I was responsible for carrying out the work of the ministry.

The attitude that "this is best left to the professionals" is one of two concepts that tend to cripple churches and Sunday Schools at the point of growth. The other is the attitude that since salvation is a free gift, there is no need for the Christian to serve. Salvation does not have to be earned. Such an idea, of course, is foreign to a proper understanding of salvation (See Ephesians 2:8-9 and James 2:14-18) The bottom line is this: Every believer – every Sunday School class member – is a minister. We are called to lives of humble, obedient service. Are your members willing to pay the price to serve?

## 7 The cost of stepping outside one's comfort zone

Almost everything that has been said may be summed up in this last cost. Genuine discipleship requires all of us, regardless of our position in the church or level of Christian maturity, to step outside our comfort zone. We have all eternity, after all, to be comfortable. Are your members willing to pay this price?

An older church in Fort Worth had a reputation in its community for being an upper-class church for "whites only." The perception in the community was that the members didn't care about them. The new pastor was determined to change this situation. He began training his members in the exercise of their spiritual gifts. Together, they established *Touch Ministry*, the goal of which was to *Touch Fort Worth with the Love of Christ*. More than 100 members, most of whom were senior adults, became a part of Touch Ministry. Each member of the lay ministry team was to develop his or her own ministry out in the community. Some tutored school children. Others delivered food to *unchurched* bereaved families throughout the community. The youth would periodically hold a *free* car wash. The difference was that they would not accept any money for their efforts – not even donations. When asked why, they replied. *Jesus taught us to offer a cup of cold water in His name. You don't look thirsty, but you do have a dirty car.* The message spread throughout the community. Because so many members of this old, traditional church had been willing to step outside their comfort zones, the community began to see the church in an entirely new light: *The church that cares.*[5]

## *The cost to be paid by staff*

We as pastors and Christian educators[6] are partly to blame for the problems outlined above. For example, for there to be a division between "ministers" and "laity," we have had to take over the former term and use it exclusively for ourselves. Often, we have chosen to be hard-working martyrs rather than equippers. We at times look like tireless super-heros to the congregation, running this way and that way, trying to get everything done. The more biblical action on our part would be to equip members to share fully in the ministry, then to be willing to delegate to and trust those whom we've equipped. I have a friend who applied this principle in a church in Texas in a ministry that extended for more than a quarter of a century. Through equipping others, he multiplied his own ministry to the extent that the Sunday School grew to an average attendance of over 3,000. All the while, my friend had evenings at home with his family. He never missed a child's ball game, science fair, or recital for a church activity. There are indeed some costs to be paid on our part, but our families need not be part of that cost.

## 1 The cost of incarnational ministry

On the Sunday evening of His resurrection, Jesus met behind closed doors with His frightened disciples. *Just as the Father has sent me*, he told them, *I also send you.* (John 20:21, HCSB) To fully understand this verse, we must understand that the Father sent the Son to live out an incarnational ministry. The Prince of Heaven set aside His privileges to become one of us. We, too, must pay the cost of incarnational ministry.

For us, an incarnational ministry could involve simply spending time with the people who need help. It is very likely that this concept will take us out of the office and onto the streets and into the hospital corridors. Two things will happen when we engage in this sort of ministry. First, we set the example for others to follow. We cannot ask our people to do that which we are unwilling to do. Second, we take Jesus out of the Sunday School classrooms and onto the streets and at times the dark alleys – all places where, as evidenced by the Gospels, He would prefer to be.

We have created comfortable work spaces for ourselves. Many of our church buildings have nice, air-conditioned offices equipped with the latest that technology has to offer. If yours is a larger church, there is probably even a room dedicated to your "break times." I know from experience that it is possible, and even a temptation, for a minister to spend all his time right there. We use excuses such as "What if a teacher needs to contact me?" to justify our behavior. We must learn to allow technology to free us from the office to be out with the people who need us. We must be willing to pay the cost of sacrificing comfort for an incarnational ministry.

## 2 The cost of risk-taking leadership

Change involves risk. As pastors and Christian educators, our choices are simple: maintain traditional approaches or work toward transformation. Let me hasten to say that tradition is not all bad. Historically, traditional Sunday Schools have been more of a strength than a weakness. The problem is that we have seen Sunday School as an end unto itself. Sunday School is intended to be a strategy for transformation. Rather than be a place where Christian culture is enjoyed, our classes ought to have as their primary purpose preparing believers for service on the front lines.

Specifically, we must be willing to lead people to do things they've never done before. We must shift the primary responsibility for ministry to the members of every Sunday School class. In doing so, we will risk criticism. As we attempt things that have never been done before, we will risk failure. We must learn to prepare our people to serve, then trust them. We must risk not *having* to initiate or supervise every ministry.

## 3 The cost of being tough

I am a veteran of a number of "battles" with deacons and other church members over my ministry style. Here are some suggestions.

First, be sure that you're on the right side. It is imperative that pastors and Christian educators spend time daily with God, meditating on His word and seeking His wisdom. Become a genuine student of the New Testament. Learn who the *real* Jesus is. Learn how He ministered to people. Learn how He risked criticism and official opposition to do what was right. You are a part of His body. Try to be sure you lead the church to do what Christ would do if He were here in a physical form.

Second, if you're not the pastor, seek to be in union with the pastor in all ministry-related issues. If you are the pastor, seek to build a team consisting of paid or lay staff who can be in harmony with you.

Third, be tough when necessary. Early in my church staff ministry, I brought together a team of people who started a bus ministry that reached into a low-income, multi-ethnic community. Nearly fifty children and teenagers poured off the bus every Sunday morning into our upper-middle class white church in Dallas. Needless to say, most of the children and teens were a little rough around the edges. Hardly a Sunday went by that a deacon in that church didn't try to force me to bring that ministry to an end: *Those kids are tearing up our church, and they don't belong here.* It would have been wrong for me to have turned aside from Christ's leadership and Scripture's teaching to follow the orders of a few deacons who were acting out of self-interest. Admittedly, there are dangers to being tough. It could even mean losing your job. If that happens, you will need to hold dear your calling, shake the dust off your feet, and move on. Are you willing to pay that price?

## *What are our options?*

I am frequently asked how traditional members of very traditional churches can be led to do the things I've suggested and will continue to suggest in this book. I'm the first to acknowledge the near impossibility of making all the changes needed within many traditional churches. Let me mention four basic approaches:

- *Tweaking the Traditional.* In this approach, we don't try to change a great deal. We simply try to improve the quality of what we have always done. Stronger Sunday Schools and more effective Bible study will result. Because of that, growth will be experienced and people will be reached.

- *The Complete Overhaul.* In this approach, the traditional church is turned into a seeker-friendly one. Most of the old traditions are eliminated. The worship services are changed to something radically different and are devoid of things meaningful only to Baptists. In most instances, the program organizations cease to exist and are replaced by more innovative strategies. Most traditional churches are not ready for such a move. In some instances, churches have been torn apart by pastors and educators who push the changes.

- *Starting from Scratch.* Many have therefore seen the futility of trying to change the unchangeable. The solution for some is to abandon the traditional approaches outright and to plant a seeker-friendly church from the ground up. This trend gained popularity in the 90s and will continue well into the 21$^{st}$ century.

- *The Blended Ministry Church.* In many parts of the country, it seems that the best hope would lie in combining the advantages of the first two approaches. Let me explain. Blended ministry churches would have a rather traditional look. They would be attractive to Christians of all ages who know the value of traditional Sunday School and who feel at home in worship services that involve pew cushions, worship bulletins, organs, and Lottie Moon announcements. But those churches would not stop there. Specialized teaching units would be designed to function in non-traditional places and at non-traditional times. A host of ministries would be established throughout the community. These ministries would operate under the authority of the church and its leaders until such times as new congregations might emerge.

*Examine these approaches carefully. Which do you believe might be the best for your ministry?*

## *The cost of doing nothing*

The only cost greater than those previously mentioned in this chapter is the cost of not changing, of not adapting. For some churches, the problem is complacency. For others perhaps the costs mentioned earlier are simply too great. These churches will continue on their present path, changing nothing. Their future is simply to die out. In many metropolitan areas, this is already beginning to happen. Communities change over time, and many congregations react to these changes by redirecting their focus inwardly. They begin a downward spiral from which they seldom recover. Tragically, the message they send out to their community, however unintentionally, is clear: *We don't like you and we don't care about you.*

This does not have to be the future of any church. For most traditional churches, the blended ministry approach described briefly above could be the beginning of a solution. This approach has been adopted as the principal strategy of this book. The remaining chapters contain principles whereby traditional Sunday Schools may be strengthened and even transformed. In every chapter there will be a concluding section entitled *Blended ministry*. In those sections, the principles of that chapter will be refocused and reapplied in non-traditional ways.

## *Notes*

# *Endnotes*

1. Unless otherwise noted, Scripture quotations marked HCSB have been taken from the Holman Christian Study Bible © copyright 2000 by Holman Bible Publishers. Used by permission.

2. This story was based on a personal conversation with the pastor, Gary Hilliard. A more complete version of this story is in *Fresh Encounter* by Dr. Henry Blackaby (Nashville: LifeWay Press, 1993).

3. The chart is original, and the ministry characteristics were gleaned from several readings of the four gospels. Could you add some lines to the chart?

4. This information was gleaned from Thom S. Rainer, *The Bridger Generation*. (Nashville: Broadman & Holman Publishers, 1997), pp. 7, 169.

5. The church in this illustration is Rosen Heights Baptist of Fort Worth, Texas. Information was derived from issues of its news letter and from conversations with the pastor (at that time), Dr. Forrest Pollock.

6. In this book, the term *Christian educator* will be taken to mean any senior staff member who has leadership responsibility in the educational ministry of the church, or an age division of that ministry. Included, therefore, would be staff specialists with youth, children, single adults, and senior adults, among others.

# Part 2:
# Blending Ministries

## Introduction

**Chapter 3: Possibilities for Growth and Ministry**
- The homogeneous principle
- Discovering prospects
- Conducting a people search
- Growing naturally
- Safeguarding prospect information
- Blended ministry:   Finding those generally overlooked

**Chapter 4: Organizing for Growth**
- Organization in the smaller Sunday School
- Organization in the larger Sunday School
- Blended ministry

**Chapter 5: Staffing the Organization**
- Designing leadership teams
- Leadership teams for smaller churches
- Staffing leadership teams
- Blended ministry

**Chapter 6: Becoming a Team**
- Teams bonding through training
- Teams bonding through planning
- Blended ministry

**Chapter 7: Providing Facilities and Equipment**
- Providing adequate space
- Providing additional space
- Age-level space and equipment needs
- Blended ministry

# Introduction to Part 2

## *The traditional part of blended ministry*

A blended ministry church, by definition, is one where traditional and non-traditional ministries coexist. Part 2 focuses on the "nuts and bolts" of building a strong Bible study program, whether on campus or in the community. As the Part 2 overview page suggests, these next few chapters will have much to say about the traditional on-campus Bible study organization. Chapter three is about discovering people who should be reached for Bible study in either setting. Chapter four emphasizes the type of organization necessary to contain that growth. Without leadership, organization is nothing more than a chart on the wall. Chapter five, therefore, deals with the development of leadership teams necessary to bring the organization to life and carry out its kingdom purposes. In chapter six, planning and training will be presented as essential ingredients in helping teams to come together and bond. Finally, space and equipment needs will be discussed in chapter seven. An attempt has been made throughout these chapters to reflect the current Sunday School guidelines presented by the staff of LifeWay Christian Resources and by experienced Sunday School leaders throughout the nation. It must be understood that Southern Baptist Sunday School leaders had in mind the application of these guidelines in traditional Bible study settings. Suggestions will be given for using or adapting those guidelines in non-traditional settings.

## *The blended ministry churches*

Throughout the remaining chapters of this book you will be introduced to blended ministry churches. Blended ministry churches are at their heart traditional churches that use time-proven methods of reaching and teaching people. You'll see a great deal in these remaining chapters that will help you to strengthen these traditional, on-campus approaches.

At the same time, blended ministry churches have a heart for the lost where they might be found. They are not prejudiced, but at the same time they realize not all people will come to them. They must, therefore, find ways to deliver "church" to the people in their own settings. To put it another way, blended ministry churches use traditional and non-traditional methods in reaching, evangelizing, and discipling people. As you review principles by which the more traditional Sunday School organization might be strengthened, you'll begin to see how some of these same principles might apply in non-traditional and off-campus Bible study settings.

You'll be introduced to five blended ministry and non-traditional churches on the next few pages. Two of these ministries, City Church of Amarillo, Texas, and Mission Arlington, are not actually blended ministry churches by our definition. Rather, they are churches designed from the ground up to reach into low-income and racially mixed communities. They are included because their ministries provide good models for blended ministry approaches.

A final word: As you are introduced to blended ministry churches and their non-traditional ministries, some of your ideas of what constitutes a church may be challenged. In reality, many of our ideas *need* to be challenged. For now, let's meet some of those churches.

# 1. First Baptist Church of Tulia, Texas:
## A prison ministry that works

First Baptist Church of Tulia, Texas, is a very traditional farming community church of some 1450 members and an average Sunday School attendance of just under 350. If you looked at their published record of annual baptisms, you probably wouldn't be impressed. The official statistics don't tell very much of the story, however. The church is a thoroughly committed missionary congregation. Over the past fifteen years, they have sent approximately twenty volunteer evangelism teams to Recife, Brazil. Hundreds have come to know Christ through the witness of these volunteers.

Nine years ago, another mission field opened up. This one happened to be just outside of town. The Tulia Transfer Facility (also known as the Swisher County Detention Center) opened in 1992 as a 600-bed medium security prison for men. Pastor Charles Davenport visited with the warden the day the prison opened. He requested permission to lead a Monday evening worship service for the inmates. Permission was granted. A deacon from the church volunteered his services as chaplain, and still others came out to serve as counselors and musicians for the services.

**Pastor Charles Davenport awarding a Bible to the first graduate of the correspondence Bible course offered through First Baptist Church of Tulia, Texas.**

The results of this ministry have been astounding. Almost 200 men are involved in the Monday evening worship services. This service has grown so large that the men must

Pastor Charles Davenport with cards representing more than 1500 professions of faith through the Tulia prison ministry.

attend alternate weeks due to the size of the common room. In addition, fifty men attend Davenport's Sunday morning Bible class – actually the church's largest Sunday School class. The most recent addition to the prison ministry is the weekly Bible correspondence course offered through the church in which just over 100 men are enrolled. These numbers tell only part of the story: *Over the past nine years, more than 1500 inmates have been led to Christ and baptized through this ministry.* The maximum length of stay there is two years. That means that approximately one in three prisoners have been led to Christ and baptized through the prison ministry of First Baptist Church! Some of these men have been allowed to come to First Baptist Church and stand in the pulpit and share a testimony of thanks to God for allowing them to be incarcerated at the Tulia prison, because it was there that they were introduced to Christ's love.[1]

## 2. City Church of Amarillo, Texas

### A "cooperative" ministry to children

In 1996, Don Lane, the pastor of Crestmont Baptist Church of Burleson, Texas, was a desperate man. He was always exhausted, he couldn't remember even simple things, and his skin was turning yellow. All this had been going on for ten years, and he didn't know why. Don's doctors eventually discovered that he had hepatitis type C and that he was in the final stages of liver failure. He resigned his church and moved to his home town of Amarillo, Texas. His medical insurance company canceled his coverage, and without insurance he felt that his chances of a transplant would be next to zero. God prompted a team of doctors at Baptist Hospital in Oklahoma City to accept him into their program. A nurse at the hospital died suddenly, and Don had his new liver and his life back.

It took all that to get Don's attention and to refocus the direction of his ministry. He and his family were destitute and without a place to life. He discovered an abandoned warehouse in downtown Amarillo that had been a home for indigents. He applied to the owner for permission to live in an upstairs apartment if he would clean it up. By this time, God had begun to place on Don's heart the downtown area of Amarillo, and particularly the children who lived nearby. He worked out another agreement with the building's owner who was impressed with the hard work Don and his family had put in. Essentially, the building was theirs if they would clean it up and renovate it. With the help of Texas Baptist Men, they did. During this process, God led Don to begin a ministry with children. Using his last $13 in food stamps, he purchased candy and ice cream and passed the word through the community. The children came, and City Church was born.

Pastor Don Lane of Amarillo's City Church

Since 1966, City Church in the heart of downtown Amarillo has operated as the hub of a ministry involving nine locations throughout the city. These include two Hispanic congregations and a number of Anglo groups. These meet either in church buildings deeded over to City Church by more traditional congregations not wishing to be involved in inner-city ministry, or in other donated facilities. One, a former nurses' dormitory, is home to *My Father's House*, a residence for twenty-eight unwed mothers and their thirty or so children.

City Church is about reaching children, leading them to Christ, and providing for their physical and spiritual needs. During the summer months, for example, City Church provides more than 500 lunches daily for these children during the absence of the school lunch program. They provide transportation for weekly Bible study and worship and for the "Kids' Express," a weekly fun-oriented Bible club. In many ways, City Church raises these children. They provide them with clothing and shoes, money for athletic fees and field trips, and even musical instruments for those who want to be in band. Many children have been with them for the entire five years and have come to love the Lane family as their own. As they become teenagers, they are further discipled through youth camps and ministries. The concept is simply to grow up a generation of strong Christians from the inner city.

Perhaps you've noticed that City Church is not really a "blended ministry" church, but rather one planted with the intention of reaching the children of the inner city. It is actually a cooperative effort in that hundreds of volunteers come from Amarillo churches and from mission teams throughout the nation. Financial help comes from hundreds of individuals and churches throughout Texas, the nation, and the world.[2]

## 3. Immanuel Baptist of Shawnee, Oklahoma

### A New Testament pattern of reaching Hispanics

Immanuel Baptist Church of Shawnee is a thoroughly missions-minded congregation as evidenced by strong financial giving and a strong track record of volunteer involvement in overseas missions. In January 2000, a three-year partnership ended between Immanuel and the Rosario Baptist Association of Argentina. This partnership resulted in some two dozen congregations and preaching points coming into existence and in hundreds professing faith in Christ. Seven mission teams of twenty to thirty members each were involved in this partnership. This writer led six of these seven trips.

The lives of those participating were forever changed. More than a dozen committed their lives to international missions. Practically everyone came back with the desire to start a Spanish-speaking work in their own community. Early in 2001, Mark and Mary Fuller, International Mission Board missionaries to Panama, indicated an interest in starting a Hispanic work in Shawnee.

**Missionaries Mark and Mary Fuller, Hispanic church planters for Immanuel, Shawnee**

There is a very traditional way to start a mission. It involves a mother church establishing a missions committee, providing space for worship and Bible study (perhaps in its own building), calling a mission pastor, and supporting that pastor as he invites persons in the community to attend. The Hispanic congregation will then grow and assume more and more of the financial responsibility of supporting its pastor and program.

Some problems are inherent in this model. *First*, the persons being reached learn that "church" is a place to come to before they learn it is a fellowship of believers. *Second*, they learn that church is a "spectator sport." They "go" to church to watch and listen as leaders do things – preach, teach, lead the singing, and so forth. *Finally*, and largely because of these first two problems, they never mature to the point that they can provide for their own facilities and their own pastor. In short, they sometimes never become a church, particularly if they are a low-income congregation.

The mission being established through Immanuel will in no way be "traditional." Church planters / missionaries Mark and Mary Fuller will assume the role of missionary rather than pastor. They will progress through a series of steps over a period of two years:

1. They will learn the culture of the local Hispanic community.

2. They will develop key contacts within that community who can open doors into homes.

3. From these contacts, homes will be opened up for cell-group Bible study and worship.

4. From the beginning, Hispanics who come to the house-church meetings will assume responsibility for finances. As quickly as possible, believers will become teachers and leaders. Every member of the group will be introduced to a ministry according to his or her gifts and interests.

5. Every member will have some responsibility for outreach to their friends and neighbors. When the group reaches a size of 15-20, the cell will divide and form two cells / house churches.

6. From a network of these house churches, worship rallies could be held, and a larger congregation could emerge. Within the two year period, the missionaries will lead them in the direction of becoming an autonomous, indigenous congregation.

At the time of this writing, the new Hispanic work at Immanuel is in its infancy. Missionaries Mark and Mary Fuller have assembled a church planting team of Spanish speaking individuals from the mother church to assist them. The church planting team meets weekly for strategy planning and prayer. They have begun developing the key contacts that will lead to invitations into homes for Bible studies. Initially, members of the church planting team will lead the Bible studies. As quickly as possible, leadership responsibilities will be turned over to Hispanic believers. No name has been selected for the new work because the missionaries feel that it's not their decision to make.[3]

It is difficult when using the cell-group approach to chart a five-year growth plan. Will the cell groups simply multiply and a network of house churches result? Will they come together to form a single congregation with a more traditional look? Will they ever be ready to purchase property and construct a building? The church planting team is waiting to see how God moves within the Hispanic community. The future of this work belongs to God.

# 4. Mission Arlington, Arlington Texas

## Taking church to the people

It was never Tillie Burgin's vision to reach into the heart of a large metropolitan city to touch the lives of tens of thousands of people through a network of more than 230 Bible study cell groups and a host of other social and spiritual ministries, but that's exactly what's happened. Tillie's vision was quite simple: to start an apartment house ministry. God gave her this vision because of a woman who had numerous physical, social, and spiritual needs. Tillie provided some help, then invited her to church. "Oh, no, Ms. Tillie. Isn't church for people who have their lives together? I don't have my life together yet. When I get my life together, I'll come to church."[4] It was then that Tillie Burgin knew that she must work to take church to the people. The first apartment ministry was started in August, 1986, after much prayer. Other opportunities came. One woman came in for help for food and help with her utility bills. The visit resulted in her apartment being opened for Bible study. The "curriculum" was John 3:16, and 17 people came the first Sunday to hear for the first time of God's love for them.

**Tillie Burgin, Executive Director
Mission Arlington/Mission Metroplex**

Through the years, Mission Arlington has grown dramatically. Currently, Bible study is held in more than 230 locations throughout Arlington and the Dallas-Fort Worth metroplex with a combined attendance of more than 3,700. The list of ministries is almost endless. In 2000, some 42,000 families were helped with rent, utilities, gasoline, and prescriptions. Food was given to 96,000 people, and approximately 50,000 received items of furniture. Through the clothes closet, 162,500 people were assisted with adult and children's clothing. During the summers, more than 15,000 children each week receive lunch as a substitute for the school lunch program. The "Rainbow Express" is a version of Backyard Bible Club that in 2000 reached more than 10,000 children in Arlington. This list could go on to include medical and dental clinics, transportation, day shelters, and child care.

Like City Church, Mission Arlington is not really a "blended ministry." Actually, it is the result of hundreds of blended ministry churches reaching out through financial and volunteer support. Literally hundreds of churches and thousands of individuals together provide the $1 million-plus needed each year. Ms. Tillie supervises a volunteer staff in excess of 2,000, each of whom she has personally interviewed and approved. These volunteers represent dozens of area churches. In addition, thirty-one full time summer missionaries assisted in 2000, and more than 100 youth and adult mission teams assisted with these ministries.

## 5. *South Georgia Baptist Church of Amarillo, Texas*

### *A model for starting apartment ministries*

Minister of Education Carey Jones had a burden to extend the ministries of his church into an apartment community in his city. The studies he had done indicated that 95% of apartment dwellers were unchurched. The numerous apartment complexes near his church provided a vast mission field. The "Timbers" apartment complex was selected for the ministry.

The vision was not for Carey Jones to carry out personally. He was called to the staff of a church in Palestine, Texas. The actual ministry was begun by Barry Robinson, a Mission Service Corps volunteer and member of the South Georgia church.

The first step was obtaining permission from the apartment complex manger. After recent vandalism, she was particularly interested in the activities that would be provided for school age children. She gave her consent for the group to use the club room.

Interest was generated through use of a survey and through a Saturday barbeque and carnival for the residents. The survey had revealed a great deal of interest in residents coming together as a community and in Bible study. The carnival provided an opportunity to publicize the first service to be held the next day, Easter Sunday of 2001.

Since its beginning, the ministry has grown to an attendance of 25 to 30. Bible study is provided for all ages. A June, 2001, Vacation Bible School involved approximately fifty children and was led by one of the resident members of the cell group. There are plans for the ministry to make a permanent home for themselves by renting an apartment to be designated as a chapel for the cell group. Barry Robinson and his wife are seeking ways to develop leadership from within the group and to expand the ministry to other apartments.[5]

These non-traditional ministries are examples of what many churches are beginning to do. You'll read more of these and other ministries in the remaining chapters of this book. As you do, begin praying for a vision of ways that you and your congregation might take Bible study to people wherever they might be.

## Endnotes

1. This information was obtained through numerous interviews with Charles Davenport, the pastor of First Baptist Church of Tulia, Texas, between February and July, 2001, and with officials from the Tulia Transfer Center. The writer has visited the prison services and has obtained much information through personal observation.

2. This information was gathered through phone conversations and personal visits with Don Lane, Executive Pastor of City Church, Amarillo, Texas, and with members of his family between February and July, 2001. Other information was gathered from the January and June, 2001, issues of *City Church*, a monthly newsletter of this ministry, and through personal observation and involvement with the ministry.

3. This information was obtained through visits with Missionaries Mark and Mary Fuller and through meetings with them and the mother church's missions committee during July, 2001. The writer is a member of that committee and has been assigned to coordinate a network of financial support for the missionary team.

4. Mission Arlington Website: www.missionarlington.org. From an article entitled, "The Beginning of Mission Arlington."

5. From interviews with Carey Jones, Minister of Education, Southside Baptist Church of Palestine, Texas, and Barry Robinson, Mission Service Corps Volunteer at South Georgia Baptist Church, Amarillo, Texas, conducted in July 2001.

# Chapter 3:
## Possibilities for Growth and Ministry

Before Arthur Flake could grow his hardware business in a new community, it was necessary for him to learn about his potential customers and their needs. To grow a church in any community, it is necessary to do the same.

From time to time, I ask my students in educational ministry or evangelism classes to take a look around the room and draw conclusions. Almost invariably, the response is the same. *We all look alike.* It's true. The vast majority of students in most of my ministry classes are white, and most are from middle-class backgrounds. I respond with, *Why do you think this is?* There are usually a variety of responses, but few hit the mark. The truth is, most of my students are white, middle-class because they come out of white, middle class churches. Just as my students do not represent a cross-section of young adults between the ages of 18 and 22 in our state, most of our churches do not represent a cross section of their own communities either.

In the early days of Southern Baptists, our churches were made up primarily of low-income rural people. Since that time, our predecessors have tried to provide a better life for the next generation. This held true until the early 1990's when, for the first time, it became obvious that young adults were not going to enjoy the same standard of living as their parents. The net result of 150 years of solid work ethic and the seeking of a better life is that we are no longer rural and no longer low-income. The population shifts in the communities surrounding many of our churches have meant that white middle-class people have moved out to newer communities. They have been replaced by a variety of low-income, multi-ethnic cultures and subcultures. It is becoming increasingly difficult to stay in touch with the people who need our message.

## *The homogeneous principle*

"Men like to become Christians without crossing social, linguistic, or class barriers," writes Donald McGavran.[1] McGavran and Win Arn define the homogeneous unit as "a group of people who all have some characteristic in common and feel that they belong."[2]

The homogeneous principle is fact, though one that at times comes into conflict with the inclusive nature of Christ and His gospel. There are times, for example, when the homogeneous principle can be used as an excuse for prejudice. "It wouldn't be a good idea for *those people* to come; they wouldn't feel comfortable here anyway," is a sentiment at times expressed or implied.

> *Are there individuals in your community who would not feel comfortable in your church? Who are these? What should be done?*

There are obviously two perspectives from which this principle may be evaluated: the side of the church member and the side of the unreached individual from another race or culture. When the homogeneous principle is viewed from the perspective of a person without Christ, it makes sense. The gulf between a secular world view and a biblical one is great enough. A lost person shouldn't have to adopt a new culture in order to fit in, should he? A part of the genius of the church is its capacity to adapt to every individual, race, and culture. We thus conclude that some other church would be better for *that* type of person.

At the same time, multi-cultural churches are needed in our complex world. The book of Acts provides examples of both homogeneous and multi-cultural churches. The congregations in Jerusalem and Antioch fit these categories, respectively.

A reading of the first six chapters of Acts reveals much about the Jerusalem church. It was a praying congregation. Its members were generous, "claiming nothing as their own." It was a courageous church, producing the first martyrs. It was a thoroughly evangelistic church where every member acknowledged a responsibility for spreading the gospel. The church had a problem, however -- *racial or class prejudice*. There was tension between two groups of believers: the Hellenistic Jewish believers and those believers from the more traditional Hebraic Judaism. In Acts 6, a dispute arose between these two classes over the treatment of Hellenistic widows. The dispute was settled, and the church continued to grow.

The real difficulty came when the church faced the dilemma of whether or not to accept Samaritan and Gentile converts. When Philip preached in Samaria, Peter and John were sent to check things out (Acts 8:4-25). When Peter shared the gospel with Cornelius and his household, he had to give an account of his actions to the church in Jerusalem (Acts 11:1-18). In that same chapter, believers left Jerusalem because of persecution and traveled northward, preaching the gospel to *no one but the Jews*. Later, when a church was established in Antioch which consisted of both Jewish and Gentile Christians, Barnabas was sent out by the Jerusalem church as a one-man investigating committee. And still later, when Paul and Barnabas finished their first mission to the Gentiles, they gave a report to the Jerusalem Council (Acts 15) which prompted a policy decision. The church in Jerusalem was a homogeneous congregation.

Compare the Antioch church. The record of its establishment is found beginning in Acts 11:19. From the very beginning, it was a multi-cultural congregation, having been established by a mixture of Jewish and Gentile believers. It was thus inclusive of everyone. Its members so resembled Christ in their speech and actions that they were the first to be called Christians. They were responsive to the financial needs of others, even sending the first recorded disaster relief offering back to Jerusalem. It was a church responsive to the leadership of God's Spirit, sending Barnabas and Saul out on the first extended mission to the Gentiles.

In the first century, the Jerusalem church continued to be the church that defined both doctrine and discipline. It was, after all, the church of the apostles. The church in Antioch, however, was selected to be the mother church for the extension of the gospel into Asia Minor and Europe.

In many ways, our churches resemble the Jerusalem congregation. Certainly, many good things could be said about most of our churches. Like the Jerusalem church, however, we tend to be racially and culturally exclusive. The reality is that we live in an "Antioch" world. We therefore need "Antioch" churches that are doctrinally sound, committed to discipleship, Christ-like, and inclusive, with a passion for a lost world.

> *In what ways does your church resemble the Jerusalem church? In what ways does it resemble the Antioch church?*

The homogeneous principle is useful only when it is viewed from the standpoint of a person in another culture. When we seek to use it to justify the exclusion of others, it is wrong. Jesus *included*. We must as well.

Still, there is the reality that provision must be made for those who cannot bridge the cultural gap from either direction. Some of these provisions will be addressed in the ***Blended ministry*** section of this chapter.

## *Discovering prospects*

Back to the challenge which confronted Mr. Flake's hardware business. He needed to learn as much as he could about his potential customer base, and he needed to know their needs. How else could he meet those needs and grow a thriving business? How else can our

Sunday Schools grow unless we learn about the unreached people all around us? For our purposes, a Sunday School prospect will be defined as someone who is not involved in Bible study on a regular basis. Below are some basic facts about prospects.

- One need not be aware that he is a prospect for Bible study in order to actually be one.

- One need not be interested in Bible study, church attendance, or the Christian faith in order to be a prospect.

- The best prospects are those we know enough about to be able to make an informed visit. Specifically, we ought to know their name, their address, their general age, and something about their Christian experience (or lack thereof). It would also be helpful to know something of their family members.

Most churches have access to a wide range of prospects. We tend to give special attention to those who are actually seeking us out. Others, we tend to ignore. Perhaps it would be helpful to look at the entire range of prospects. Consider these categories:

- ***Interested, seeking***. These are very likely the people who have already visited your church. Typically, they are Baptists looking for a church home. This is normally the group easiest to visit. Seldom do these visits become opportunities for evangelism.

- ***Mildly interested, related***. These are people who have some connection with your church through their children or through participation in a recreational event or some other "public" activity. They are slightly positive concerning your church but just haven't gotten around to visiting. They tend to respond when genuine interest is shown by Christians their age.

- ***Disinterested, related.*** Similar to the group above, these are the individuals who give permission for their children to attend, but who have no interest in being involved personally. Frequently, they have had an earlier unpleasant experience with a church. They convey the message that religion, for them, is not important. The best witness to these individuals could come through loving their children and building up a relationship of trust. In my present church, I began picking up three brothers from a home in the community on Wednesday nights for our Royal Ambassador program. Their mother allowed them to come, with the provision that we wouldn't *send the preacher* to

> *How would your approach differ for each of these groups?*

*Page 44*

visit her. We honored that request. We worked with her sons over a period of many months. When trust was established with their mother, a victory was won. It was exciting to watch her and her three sons being baptized in the same service. A significant number of evangelistic prospects will turn up in this group, but patience is required.

- **Neutral, unrelated.** These are the individuals who have no present connection to your church and have never given your church a great deal of thought one way or the other. This is a large group, with tremendous evangelistic potential.

- **Disinterested, unrelated.** This group is perhaps the hardest to reach. These individuals have gotten a rather negative impression of your church, of Baptists, or of religion in general. You will have to work hard to earn the right to be heard.

- **Unknown.** This is perhaps the largest group of all. You do not know their names, you don't know anything about their level of interest, and you know nothing about their spiritual experience. They live all around you but may be invisible to you.

## Two Basic Methods of Prospect Discovery

Wisdom based on much experience suggests that you build a prospect file of names equal to the number of individuals on your Sunday School roll. This will provide a steady stream of prospects for your visitation and evangelism programs. There are many ways of discovering prospects. I would like to group those methods into two categories.

**1** *Those unaware that they have been discovered*
This category consists of individuals for whom we have some time to prepare and develop strategies for outreach, ministry, and evangelism. Since they are not aware that we are interested in them, they will not be expecting a contact right away. This gives us a little time to develop our contacts with them. Common sources of information for this category include:

- Newcomers list (or new meter connections)
- Birth announcements in newspaper
- Church members who are not enrolled in Sunday School
- Family members of church or Sunday School members
- Referrals by church members

*Can you think of other sources of prospect information that fit this category?*

Certainly, other sources of prospect information could be added to this list. We might have very limited information for some of these prospects. A census-type visit might be in order to provide enough information to assign them to a visitation team.

## 2 *Those aware that they have been discovered*

The clock is ticking for this group. They know that we know about them. They might or might not be interested in our church, but they are nevertheless *expecting* to hear from us. Information discovered about prospects in ways that involve their knowledge has a very limited shelf-life.

I learned this the hard way. While teaching at another university, I served on a part-time basis as minister of education of a church in Texas. The church was located in a farming community of approximately 5,000. When I first started my ministry there, I found no prospect file. I wanted to do what came naturally -- conduct a People Search (to be discussed later). My Sunday School leaders wouldn't even think about my proposal. *Absolutely not!* was the chorus of responses I got. These were good, dedicated people, and I naturally wanted to know why. *Have you looked over in the boxes in the corner of your office?* I hadn't up until that time, but with the help of the church secretary, I started going through them. The boxes contained census cards completed in a massive People Search project. Virtually every house in town had been surveyed. The People Search had taken place two years previously, and the cards had not been touched since that time. The message sent out by the Baptist church to every resident in the community was unmistakable: *We now know who you are, and we really don't care about you!* Many of the people who had been contacted by our members under the direction of my zealous predecessor had expected a follow-up visit. They received none.

*How does it make you feel when you think someone doesn't care about you? Do you enjoy being ignored?*

Here's the lesson: When employing one of the methods listed below, *do so only at the rate at which you are able to incorporate them into your regular visitation program.* This may mean that to bring your prospect file up to the size of your Sunday School roll, time may be required. Here are some sources of information:

- People Search (neighborhood canvass)
- Registration at block party, concert, or other community event
- Filling out a visitor's card in Sunday School or worship
- Block-watchers (where an actual contact has been made)
- VBS parents (where information was obtained from parents)
- Other children's or youth programs, including bus ministry
- Use of direct mail with response cards
- Telephone surveys
- Can you think of others?

# Conducting a people search

The People Search, or door-to-door religious survey, remains one of the most useful methods for discovering prospect information. The basic purpose of the People Search is to obtain specific information concerning residents in your community who are in need of Bible study, a church home, an evangelistic visit, or other specific ministries. At the very least, the People Search should yield the following information: name, address, approximate age, names and ages of family members, and the need for Bible study. Other helpful information might include spiritual condition, telephone number, and/or occupation. Some People Searches may be specialized to do the following: distribute Scripture, share the gospel, obtain ministry needs or suggestions, or offer prayer support

## Figure 4
## Steps to Conducting a People Search

1. Determine a date *at least six weeks in advance*. Often, a target date can be set in preparation for a future event such as a revival or dedication of a new building.
2. Determine a survey approach: *census information, Scripture distribution, prayer needs, ministry needs, evangelistic, etc.*
3. Determine the number of prospective family units which could be followed up on within a month to six weeks. *Remember that the information is almost totally useless after this period of time.*
4. Determine a survey area and size. *A team of two workers can reasonably survey 20 to 25 homes within two hours. On the average, each assignment will yield approximately three prospect family units.* To obtain the number of homes, use this formula:
   **Prospect units needed x 10 = Number of homes in survey area**
5. Determine number of people search teams needed
   **Number of homes in survey area ÷ 20**
6. Design and duplicate (or purchase) needed survey materials.
   *Information cards, envelopes, instruction sets, maps, etc.*
7. Promote the event in your church and enlist teams. *Enlist group captains personally, and enlist canvassers using sign-up cards.*
8. Enlist the support staff to handle record keeping, food preparation, and child care.
9. Train the workers. *Generally, this is done on the day you go out.*
10. Conduct the survey. *It is important that the pastor or other People Search leader take an assignment.*
11. Provide a report-back session during which time cards are returned.
12. Plan a testimony session during an evening worship service.
13. Transfer the prospect information onto visitation assignment cards as quickly as possible.

Common advantages of the People Search include:

1. Fairly thorough coverage of a wide area of your community
2. Discovery of information concerning a significant number of people who are not involved in Bible study anywhere
3. Information concerning ministry or prayer needs
4. Ability to target specific neighborhoods and systematic coverage of larger population areas over a period of time
5. Up-close demographic information
6. Opportunities for members to see the needs around the church first-hand
7. Opportunities to share information about your church and its ministries
8. Opportunities for supporting future outreach, ministry, and evangelistic efforts.

## *Growing naturally*

Jerusalem was filled with the teachings of Christ. The Lord added to the church (in Jerusalem) on a daily basis those who were being saved. Everyone in Asia Minor had an opportunity to hear the good news of Christ. Many other examples such as these from Acts could be found. What do they have in common? *More than likely, none of them used prospect files.* How, then, did the growth take place? The answer is growth through natural relationships.

Here's a more contemporary example: A university president and former pastor told of going to a new pastorate. He arrived on the church field just in time for the annual meeting of the nominating committee. He listened as names were suggested for several teaching positions in the Sunday School. For a young women's class, the name of a Vietnamese woman was suggested. The new pastor had already met the woman. She was pleasant, but her accent was very difficult to understand. He suggested that she might not be a wise choice because of her heavy accent. The members of the nominating committee were insistent and the new pastor didn't object. He decided to watch the class closely, however.

> *Would your adult class members be willing to invite their best friend to attend their class? If not, why not?*

Soon after the Vietnamese teacher started, her class began to grow. Within a few weeks, they needed a larger room. The pastor continued to monitor the progress of the class. Within a month or so, yet another room was needed. The pastor's curiosity got the best of him. One Sunday morning, he stood outside the classroom. The first words out of the teacher's mouth were, "OK, girls, get out your homework. Let's see what you've done."

This class didn't grow by visiting names on a prospect file. It grew because its members were having their needs met by the quality of Bible study taking place. They invited their friends and neighbors. Some Sunday Schools have found that this type of word-of-mouth advertising is best. As people grow through quality Bible study, they simply invite their friends. Quality is essential: Who would want to invite a friend to something they would be embarrassed about? Generally, the outreach visits are unscheduled and informal.

Natural growth through casual relationships will generally follow homogeneous principles, and it may therefore not be especially effective in reaching minorities or members of other socio-economic groups. For that reason, natural growth should be supplemented with other prospect discovery methods.

## *Safeguarding prospect information*

A prospect file is as important to a Sunday School as a customer list is to a salesman. Once prospect information has been obtained, it is essential to have a plan for safeguarding and utilizing it. Let's look at some basic elements of the plan:

1. ***Safeguarding Information*** – A good prospect file should be kept safe. This requires a central storage system in which an original copy of the information is kept. The original should never leave the office. At the same time, it should be accessible, since it needs to be updated continually. Assignment copies will be made from the original. There are several methods:
   - A computer file (with electronic or hard copy backup)
   - A photocopy of a card in a 3-ring binder organized by age groups
   - A permanent sleeve (or envelope) which is kept in a binder. The insert card is made available for assignment, but never the envelope. A binder is available for each department or age group.
   - An index card file
   - A master printed list

2. ***Making information available*** – Prospect assignment cards should be made available whenever Sunday School workers and members are in the building. The primary times of availability should be the regular weekly outreach time, on Sunday mornings in the Sunday School class, and on Wednesday evenings. In addition, assignment cards ought to be available in the office for drop-ins.

3. **Updating information** – At the very least, prospect assignment cards should contain the following information: Name, address, phone (if available), age (or general age), and the source of the information (church member, visitor, People Search, etc.) Provision must be made for updating the information to add names of family members and to add notes related to progress, interest, and suggestions for future visits. This is sometimes easier said than done. Two basic suggestions will help. First, someone must be assigned to receive the information and update the file. Second, there must be a convenient way for visitation teams members to turn in reports of their visits. Consider these possibilities:
   - A report-in time (workable only with regular visitation times)
   - A report-in place, such as a locked box outside the church office
   - Report in by telephone
   - Mail prospect cards by way of a pre-addressed envelope to the church office.

4. **Addition of new prospect information** – It should be the responsibility of an outreach secretary, paid or volunteer, to regular convert raw data (visitor's card, People Search survey card) to a prospect assignment card.

5. **Deletion of obsolete information** – Surprisingly, this is usually the easiest but one of the most neglected jobs of all. It is important to keep prospect rolls up to date to avoid the discouragement that comes from visiting members of other churches, persons who have moved, or those who have joined your church. They should not be removed simply because there is no apparent interest, but referred to a more highly trained "care team."

## Blended ministry: Finding those generally overlooked

*The scroll of the prophet Isaiah was given to Him, and unrolling the scroll, He found the place where it was written: "The Spirit of the Lord is upon Me, because He has anointed Me to preach the good news to the poor. He has sent Me freedom for the captives and recovery of sight to the blind, to set free the oppressed, and to proclaim the year of the Lord's favor." He then rolled up the scroll, gave it back to the attendant, and sat down. The eyes of everyone in the synagogue were fixed on Him. He began "Today this Scripture has been fulfilled in your hearing." (Luke 4:17-21, HCSB)*

Are there persons or groups in your community "poor, blind, or imprisoned?" Are there groups or classes of people who are not attending your church and probably not attending any church? Use the chart in Figure 5 to begin the process of finding unreached people. Note: The chart is not intended to suggest individuals or groups which should not be included in the traditional ministries of your church.

### Discovery Tools

I have served on the staff of a number of upper-middle-class churches in older neighborhoods. These churches and many others have one thing in common: *The people on the outside differ greatly from those on the inside.*

I was in my first staff church in a low income community just north of downtown Dallas. I was convinced that the people on the inside must evidently drive to church with blinders on. They drove through the community every Sunday, but they didn't see it. With my pastor's permission and a 35-millimeter camera, I took action. One Sunday morning while we were having Sunday School and the morning worship service at our church, I photographed the community through a telephoto lens. I got it all: "street urchins" playing in gutters, beer-bellied middle-aged men sitting out on front porches surrounded by empty cans, yards piled high with litter. Even I was amazed at the number of people I saw. I'll confess that although I had visited in that community for several months, that morning they looked as strange to me as the folks in our church must have looked to them.

I didn't stop there. With another roll or two of film, I took pictures of what was happening on the inside of our church the following Sunday. I put the two sets of pictures together with music – sounds of an organ playing an anthem, mixed with the music and noise of the streets. It was a sermon without words. I played it the following Sunday evening. After the 15-minute media presentation, I had a line of people waiting to talk with me, asking what they could do! Our people had been blind, but their hearts were touched when they began to see what Jesus saw.

And so it is in all of our churches. How can we go about helping our people to see the needs? Here are some suggestions.

**First, make sure you see the needs and that you allow your own heart to be broken.** Make your own visits. Knock on doors. Get to know your neighbors. Ask what their needs and concerns are. Pray with them on the doorstep. Learn to be shock-proof.

**Use a focused People Search.** Now that you know what to expect, help your people to see what you see. The purpose of your People

Search should be to obtain information related to prayer and ministry needs. Ask questions such as, *How could our church meet the needs of people in this community?* Compile a list. Gather some interested Sunday School workers and members and begin praying about ways to meet those needs.

**Use demographic studies to help discover population trends and community characteristics.** Some of this information is probably available from your city's planning and zoning board. Spend a morning at city hall learning about the resources available, and plan ways to use those resources effectively. Several state conventions have planning and research services such as that in Oklahoma, led by Sam Vinal. Through offices like this one, access to information has been made available in unprecedented ways through Scan/US, a "geo-demographic software package developed by the Baptist Sunday School Board (currently LifeWay Christian Resources) in conjunction with Scan/US Inc. of California."[3] Demographic descriptors include population, population change, age groupings (expressed in terms of developmental tasks or generations), gender, race, income, education, family status, religious affiliation, and lifestyle.[4]

**Use a survey.** The survey goes beyond the People Search by seeking information related to the culture, needs, and interests of the target group. Missionaries Mark and Mary Fuller have developed such a survey to learn the culture, needs, and interests of Hispanics in Shawnee. Brian Robinson used a community interest survey with residents of the Timbers apartment complex in Amarillo, Texas. Residents were asked to check from a list of activities or classes those that would meet needs. These included ESL (English as a Second Language) classes, Bible clubs for children, CPR classes, a Latchkey Child Program, G.E.D. preparation, cooking classes, exercise/aerobic classes, and Bible study. Other questions asked why residents felt that most people didn't attend class, and what they would look for personally in a church.[5] It could also be helpful to survey members of your own congregation using a tool such as *the Informal Demographic Checklist* (Figure 5) to identify unreached populations in your community.

**Consider the institutions.** Most communities have one or more of the following institutions or services where people in need of Bible study might be found: retirement homes, adult day care centers, nursing homes, women's shelters, juvenile detention centers, and prisons. Speak with the directors or administrators of these facilities. Visit the residents (or inmates) in these locations.

# Figure 5
## *Informal Demographic Checklist*

**Instructions:** *Check all that apply (columns A, B, C, and D) using the following criteria:*

    A = Group is represented in community
    B = Group is represented in congregation or Sunday School
    C = Group which <u>could</u> be reached through traditional Sunday School
    D = Group for which there is presently a church or Bible study in community

| | A | B | C | D |
|---|---|---|---|---|
| Sunday workers | | | | |
| Teen aged high school dropouts | | | | |
| Single / divorced parents | | | | |
| Unmarried couples | | | | |
| Families on welfare | | | | |
| Families in mobile home parks / low income housing | | | | |
| Released felons / parolees | | | | |
| Current or former prostitutes | | | | |
| Current or recovering alcoholics / drug users | | | | |
| Ethnic / language groups: | | | | |
|     Native American | | | | |
|     Hispanic | | | | |
|     Black | | | | |
|     Asian | | | | |
|     Middle Eastern | | | | |
| Other | | | | |
| Other: | | | | |

**Look for the "worst first."** This is the operating philosophy of City Church of Amarillo, Texas. This concept has led them to minister to drug addicts, prostitutes, and the homeless. Students at Baylor University have participated in "Church Under the Bridge," an outside "chapel" for the homeless and hobos who sleep under the Interstate 35 bridges in and near Waco, Texas. Imagine Jesus walking the inner city streets and alleys of your community. Where would He go to find the hopeless? With whom would He speak? You, after all, are Christ's presence in these places.

**Spend time in the community you're trying to reach.** Don Lane and his family chose to live in the second floor of the warehouse that would be home to City Church in Amarillo. He commented, "I could live in one of the newer residential areas of Amarillo, but my ministry wouldn't be the same. People wouldn't trust me as much."[6] When developing an off-campus ministry, such as a Bible study in an apartment community, consider leasing an apartment where the cell group leaders or hosts would live. In any event, spend as much time as possible where your target group lives. Shop in their grocery stores and purchase gasoline at their stations. Get to know them personally, and *let them see you there.* The term for this is *incarnational ministry.* Jesus' incarnational ministry involved His willingness to leave His world to walk in ours. He laid aside the privileges and glory associated with being the Prince of Heaven to live as a common man. Jesus didn't live among us as a member of the cultural elite, or as part of the upper-class of society. Rather, He chose to be born in a place for animals. He grew up as part of a lower-class family. He was a carpenter, a man who worked with His hands. Throughout His ministry, He owned no home. It was said of Him that He had no place to lay His head. He taught from no great Temple or synagogue; rather, he taught on hillsides and by river banks, beside wells and along dusty streets. He said to His disciples and to us, "*As the Father has sent me, so send I you.*" (John 20:21)

> *Which of these techniques have you used to learn about your community? Are there other techniques you would suggest?*

Whatever the specific method, it is only through incarnational ministry that we can learn what we need to learn in order to teach people of any circumstance and to minister to their needs. As you obtain information through one or more of the sources listed above, begin to organize what you have come to learn about your community. Begin to identify some priority needs as well as possibilities for non-traditional Bible study groups. You'll read in later chapters of this book about ways to plan, organize, enlist and train workers, and provide curriculum for these studies.

# Notes:

# Endnotes

1. Donald A. McGavran, *Understanding Church Growth* (Grand Rapids: William B. Eerdmans Publishing Company, 1970), p. 198.

2. Donald A. McGavran and Win Arn, *Ten Steps for Church Growth* (New York: Harper and Row, Publishers, 1977), p. 129.

3. Sam Vinal, *A Guide to Using Demographic Data to Reach People.* © 1977 by Sam H. Vinal, 2$^{nd}$ edition 1998, p. 1.

4. Ibid, pp. 6-12.

5. From the "Timbers" Community Interest Survey (unpublished) developed by Brian Robinson, Mission Service Corps Volunteer at South Georgia Baptist Church in Amarillo, Texas. It was first used at the Timbers in April, 2001.

6. From a conversation with Don Lane, Executive Pastor of City Church, on July 22, 2001.

# Chapter 4:
## Organizing for Growth

Arthur Flake learned that knowing his field of prospective customers was not enough. He had to prepare to meet their needs. For the hardware business, it meant developing a sales organization and an inventory plan. For his Sunday School, it meant organizing new classes and departments.

Let's briefly review the terminology of organization:

- **Class** = This is the basic teaching unit for adults and youth in Sunday Schools of all sizes and for preschoolers and children in smaller Sunday Schools. The minimum requirement for a class is a group of learners with a teacher.

- **Department** = For adults and youth and some children, the department consists of two or more classes under the leadership of a department director. For preschoolers and some children's groups, the department is a larger group of children under the leadership of a team of workers consisting of a director and an appropriate number of teachers. The "department" type of organization is generally used in medium and larger sized Sunday Schools.

- **Division** = This term has a formal and an informal meaning. Formally, "division" refers to a group of departments within a specific age grouping. For example, the Youth Division; the Senior Adult Division. Factors other than age can apply, such as the Single Adult Division. Informally, the term refers to the five basic age groupings in most churches: Preschool (birth through pre-first grade), Children (grades 1-6), Youth (grades 7-12), Young Adult (18 or married through 24), and Adult (25+).

- **Sunday School** = This is the overall organization for Bible teaching and reaching. In this book, the term *Sunday School* will refer only to Bible study in traditional Sunday morning settings. *Bible study* will refer to that study taking place in non-traditional settings and at times other than Sunday morning.

### *Figure 6*[1]
### Barnette's Laws Related to Growth

| Size of Units | Units (classes) normally reach their maximum growth within a few months after they are started. |
|---|---|
| New Units | New units grow faster and win more people to Christ and provide more workers than older units. |
| Grading | Grading by ages provides the logical basis for adding new units. |

Quickly review Barnette's laws related to Sunday School growth (Figure 6). These laws were developed in the 40s and 50s. Churches that followed them experienced unprecedented growth in the 60s and 70s. *Do these laws still work?* The answer is *yes*. They are just as applicable in growing Sunday Schools today as they ever were. A more difficult question might be *why?* The best answer comes by observing older, more established classes. Such classes have their own established membership roll, their own organization, and their own traditions. I've known many adult classes with their own yearbooks, treasuries, and business meetings. Such classes are very comfortable for members who enjoy the benefits of long-term relationships with close friends. It is difficult for classes like these to attract new people.

People are basically social in nature. We need a certain number of friends in our lives. When that number of friendships exists, we are content. We don't sense the need for new relationships. When the friendships do not exist or when old friendships have been broken off, we are hungry for new ones. This is the situation of many new Christians, new members, or visitors. For example, if a couple has recently moved into a new community, they've left their old friends behind and need new ones. The same is true when an adult or a teenager professes faith in Christ. If they come to a place where everyone has enough friendships, they will almost certainly have a difficult time being accepted. The addition of new units and the practice of annual promotion or age grading keeps the classes open and flexible and more willing to accept new people.

## *Organization in the smaller Sunday School*

For our purposes, the smaller Sunday School may be defined as one with an enrollment of 150 or fewer. Generally, the "class" organization rather than the "department" organization is used.

How many units (classes) are needed to facilitate growth? First look at the ratios in the chart to the right (Figure 7).[2] The enrollment maximum figure represents the recommended enrollment ceiling for each age group. The worker-pupil ratio helps determine the optimum number of workers necessary to accommodate that enrollment.

To provide an organization capable of facilitating growth, two factors should be considered: current enrollment and growth goals. The first figure is easy to obtain from current records. The second figure is established by determining a reasonable number from the prospect file that can be reached within a year. In most churches, two or more new members must be enrolled to have a net gain of one, because of attrition. The total of these two figures represents the growth potential.

***Enrollment + Growth Goals = Growth Potential***

The church represented in Figure 8 currently has a Sunday School of 120 members, with a goal to increase that enrollment to 150 within one year. It has two classes for preschoolers, two for children, one for youth, and three for adults at the

### Figure 7

**Sunday School Organization Needs**

| Age or Grade | Enrollment Maximum | Worker-Pupil Ratio |
|---|---|---|
| Babies & Ones | 9 | 1:3 |
| Two's | 12 | 1:4 |
| 3-5 | 16 | 1:4 |
| Grades 1-6 | 30 | 1:6 |
| Grades 7-12 | 12 - Class  60 - Dept | 1:8 |
| Adult | 25 - Class  125 - Dept | |

### Figure 8

| Age Divisions | Current Units (classes) | Current Enrollment | Growth Goal | Total Possibilities | Total Units Needed |
|---|---|---|---|---|---|
| Preschool | 2 | 14 | 6 | 20 | 3 |
| Children | 2 | 20 | 4 | 24 | 3 |
| Youth | 1 | 16 | 6 | 22 | 2 |
| Adults | 3 | 67 | 14 | 81 | 4 |
| General Officers | | 3 | | 3 | |
| | 8 | 120 | 30 | 150 | 12 |

current time. The size and availability of the rooms, to be dealt with in Chapter 7, must be considered, as well. Study the chart carefully. It will help in determining the number of new organizational units needed. The best times to start new classes are at the beginning of a new Sunday School year or the beginning of a new quarter, although it can be done almost any time. When dividing or re-grading adult classes, it is important to spend time with the leaders of those classes, making sure they understand the necessity for the changes.

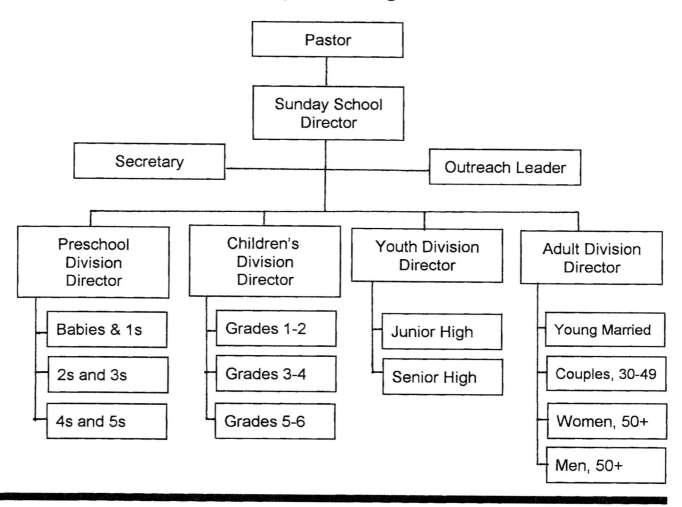

*Figure 9*
**Small Sunday School Organization**

In this organization the Preschool and Children's division directors could act as "floaters," providing help where needed. The church's youth minister / leader could serve as youth division director, and in some cases

the Sunday School director could serve also as adult division director.
More will be said in another chapter about the responsibilities of leaders.

A Sunday School of this size is ready to begin making the transition to a department-type organization, grouping classes together for purposes of fellowship, ministry, outreach, and evangelism. When is your Sunday School ready to move from a class to a department type of organization? That's a pretty subjective question, but here are some guidelines:

- When growth has halted around 150-200 in enrollment
- When preschool and children's classes are too large for one or two teachers to handle
- When there are multiple youth and adult classes that would benefit from having a common large group experience with people who are similar in age
- When facilities allow for large group and small group learning experiences
- When it is difficult to maintain fellowship between existing classes
- When greater flexibility in teaching would be desirable

The important lesson to remember is that failure to make this change can often halt growth. The movement to a department type of organization can facilitate continued growth and greater effectiveness in fellowship, ministry, and even teaching.

## *Organization in the larger Sunday School*

The larger Sunday School generally has an enrollment of 150 or more and uses the department-type organization in all age divisions.

When determining the number of units needed in this category, it's helpful to look at the big picture. Let's try something. Add together all the teaching units in your Sunday School. In churches with the department-type organization, teaching units refer to adult and youth classes and children's and preschool departments. Do you have a number? If you do, then determine the total enrollment of your Sunday School. Divide the enrollment by the number of teaching units. The result will be the ratio between units and enrollment. Figure 10 on the next page provides a model for increasing the number of teaching units to facilitate growth. Note that as new teaching units were added, the ratio between units and enrollment improved.

## Figure 10
## Determining Needs for New Units in Larger Churches

| Divisions | Departments | Current Units | Enrollment | Growth Goal | Total Possibilities | Units Needed |
|---|---|---|---|---|---|---|
| Preschool | Babies | 1 (D)* | 6 | 1 | 7 | 1 |
| | Ones | 1 (D) | 7 | 1 | 8 | 1 |
| | 2s and 3s | 1 (D) | 12 | 2 | 14 | 2 |
| | 4s and 5s | 1 (D) | 15 | 2 | 17 | 2 |
| Children | 1st Grade | 1 (D) | 15 | 2 | 17 | 1 |
| | 2nd Grade | 1 (D) | 16 | 2 | 18 | 1 |
| | 3-4 Grade | 1 (D) | 25 | 4 | 29 | 2 |
| | 5-6 Grade | 1 (D) | 28 | 4 | 32 | 2 |
| Youth | Jr High | 2 (C)** | 24 | 3 | 27 | 3 |
| | Sr. High | 3 (C) | 32 | 4 | 36 | 4 |
| Adult | A1 - 18-25 | 2 (C) | 65 | 7 | 72 | 3 |
| | A2 - 26-35 | 2 (C) | 70 | 7 | 77 | 4 |
| | A3 - 36-45 | 3 (C) | 72 | 7 | 79 | 4 |
| | A4 - 46-59 | 3 (C) | 75 | 7 | 82 | 4 |
| | A5 - 60-up | 3(C) | 80 | .8 | 88 | 4 |
| | College | 1(C) | 35 | 4 | 39 | 2 |
| | Sing Ad | 1 (C) | 25 | 3 | 28 | 2 |
| Gen Off | | | 5 | | 5 | |
| | | **27 Units** | **607** | | **675** | **42 Units** |
| Note: *(D) = Department **(C) = Class | | | **Ratio: 1:22** | | | **Ratio: 1:16** |

Here's what Sunday School growth experts have found: Declining churches characteristically have a ratio of one teaching unit per twenty-two or more enrolled (1:22). Holding pattern churches (those which are neither growing nor declining) generally have a ratio of 1:19-22. Growing churches are those with a ratio of 1:18 or less. These ratios assume that preschoolers and children are grouped by departments rather than by individual classes.

Figure 10, above, depicts the organization in a larger church with an enrollment of around 600 setting a 10% growth goal. At present, the unit to enrollment ratio is 1:22, and this is not conducive to growth. The addition of new units should bring the ratio to under 1:18. To accomplish this, a total of fifteen new classes (or departments) must be started. The addition of new teaching units (adult or youth classes, children's or preschool departments) requires a space for each new unit, and the addition of personnel. These will be dealt with in later chapters.

> *Does your units to enrollment ratio place you in the declining Sunday School category? The holding pattern? The growing Sunday School category? How many new units would be necessary to halt decline or to begin growing?*

Before leaving this section, let's think about some other Bible study units we might add as part of our on-campus Sunday School ministry. One need which almost every church has is an adult Sunday School class which meets on Sunday evening. A minister of education reported that the Sunday evening lessons were taught one week ahead of the regular schedule. This permitted the church to target three groups: [1] Adult Sunday School teachers who benefitted from a lesson preview for the coming week. [2] Teachers of youth, children, or preschoolers who seldom had the opportunity to attend an adult Bible study class. [3] Those who worked on Sunday mornings.

Topical or short-term Bible study classes could be offered on either Sunday morning or Sunday evening for groups such as leaders in training, young couples preparing for marriage, or other special interest groups. Bible study topics too advanced for the mainstream organization could be offered in this setting.

## *Blended ministry*

In conferences as well as in the classroom, I ask participants to think about the number of workers in their church or in a church with which they are familiar. I ask them to estimate the number of workers in that church. "Workers" would include just about every imaginable job, including Sunday School teachers, outreach leaders, choir members, RA or GA leaders, committee members, church officers, and deacons. Go ahead and estimate the number of workers in your church. Do you have it? Now, let's divide those workers into two lists. In one list, put those who perform all or almost all of their ministry on the church's campus. In the other list, put those who perform all or almost all of their ministry off-campus, out in the community. Have you done that? Which list is longer? By what percentage? Normally, I get responses which range from 90-95% on-campus. Think about it: Only 5-10% of our ministries are performed out where there are lost people. Doesn't that sound like a strategic blunder to you?

> **Do you see any way to strive for having 25-50% of your church's ministries performed out in the community?**

Jesus didn't mind going off-campus. In fact, that's usually where you found Him as he went about preaching, teaching, and healing. Why did He spend so much time "out of the church office?" It's simple: He went to where the people were who had needs. In the previous chapter, we considered ways of discovering these individuals and their needs. Hopefully, some potential target groups emerged which could be addressed now. In this section five possible ministries are suggested for consideration by blended ministry churches.

> **In the space in this column, list several populations groups which your church might target for outreach Bible study or one of the other approaches mentioned.**

**1. Outreach Bible Study** – These are specially focused Bible study classes which take Bible study out into the community to target those who might never attend the more traditional version. Many churches have had positive results with Bible studies in apartment complexes, mobile home parks, nursing homes, houses in low-income or racially-mixed communities, and what some are calling *city churches* – Bible studies and worship services in rented downtown buildings.

One of the most successful outreach Bible study ministries is conducted by Mission Arlington, a community missions project of First Baptist Church, Arlington, Texas. Director Tillie Burgin states, "In order to take church to the people, Bible studies are held in approximately **230** different locations throughout the city in apartment communities, mobile home parks, retirement centers, nursing homes, office buildings, and homes. Current attendance is approximately **3,700** weekly."[3]

Below are some required basic elements:

- A place and time for Bible study
- A host and/or hostess
- A teacher and other personnel (to be discussed later)
- A plan for providing ministries to meet social needs
- A curriculum plan
- An organization that facilitates coordination
- Good communication throughout the ministry
- A means of accountability to the church

**2. Extension Sunday Schools** – The basic difference between the extension Sunday School and the Outreach Bible Study is age group scope. The Outreach Bible Study generally targets adults. The extension Sunday School is for all ages. This is an ideal strategy for starting a new congregation. Consider renting space in a shopping center, school, or other building which would be available on Sunday. Extension Sunday Schools could meet in new growth areas or could be planted anywhere there is a need for a church to reach out to a demographic population being missed by existing churches. Extension Bible studies are part of the City Church strategy in Amarillo. Bible study classes are held at various times during the week in locations throughout the community as well as on Sunday morning.

**3. Prison Bible Study** – The prison ministry operated by First Baptist Church of Tulia in the Tulia Transfer Facility (a 600-bed medium security[4] prison) provides several Bible study opportunities. Sunday morning Bible study is led by the pastor and is attended by 50 to 60 inmates. These make up the church's largest Sunday School class. Davenport commented on two other unusual features of the class: First, his members virtually memorize the lesson before Sunday morning, and second, they ask far deeper questions than most Christians would. A new feature of the ministry is the Bible correspondence school (the Exodus Program) in which more than 25% of the prison population participate. Students' papers are graded by a dozen or so senior adult volunteers who add their words of encouragement.[5]

Currently, the prison population of Oklahoma is estimated to be 20,700 in state and privately owned prisons and correctional centers.[6] The opportunities for ministry within this system are practically unlimited.

**4. Impromptu Bible Study Fellowships** – The term "impromptu" is used here to mean that these groups are essentially unplanned by church leadership. They are spontaneous groups, led by individual church members who sense God's leadership to do so. Church leadership should not discourage these groups, but rather should support them through providing Bibles and other study materials. These could include Bible studies at school (before or after, but subject to school policy), at the workplace, at national parks or campgrounds, or in the homes of individual members who invite friends and neighbors into their homes. The last method listed was employed by Rick Warren's Saddleback church.[7]

The possibilities are endless: A wealthy member of the Rosen Heights Baptist Church in Fort Worth would load some old work clothes into her expensive car and head toward the local laundromat. She took extra soap and a roll of quarters and watched for women who needed help. She would provided the soap or quarters they needed, then invited them to sit down and visit with her. Often, a thirty-minute Bible study during the wash cycle and another during the dry cycle resulted.

**5. Alternative youth outreach ministry –** As an approach to Bible study, this could take place either on or off campus. The focus would be the rock music subculture of youth out on the streets. Many of these are on alcohol, drugs, or both. A surprising number are high-school dropouts who would have a hard time relating to our term, "Student Ministry"[8]. A number of churches have mixed loud music, food, and caring youth workers at a time at which most deacons and women of the Woman's Missionary Union have retired for the evening: Friday evenings from 10:00 PM - 2:00 AM seems to work for many. There's really no special secret to this type of ministry. Simply treat the kids like real people and be genuine in your concern for them.

*Figure 11*
**Extension Bible Study Organization**

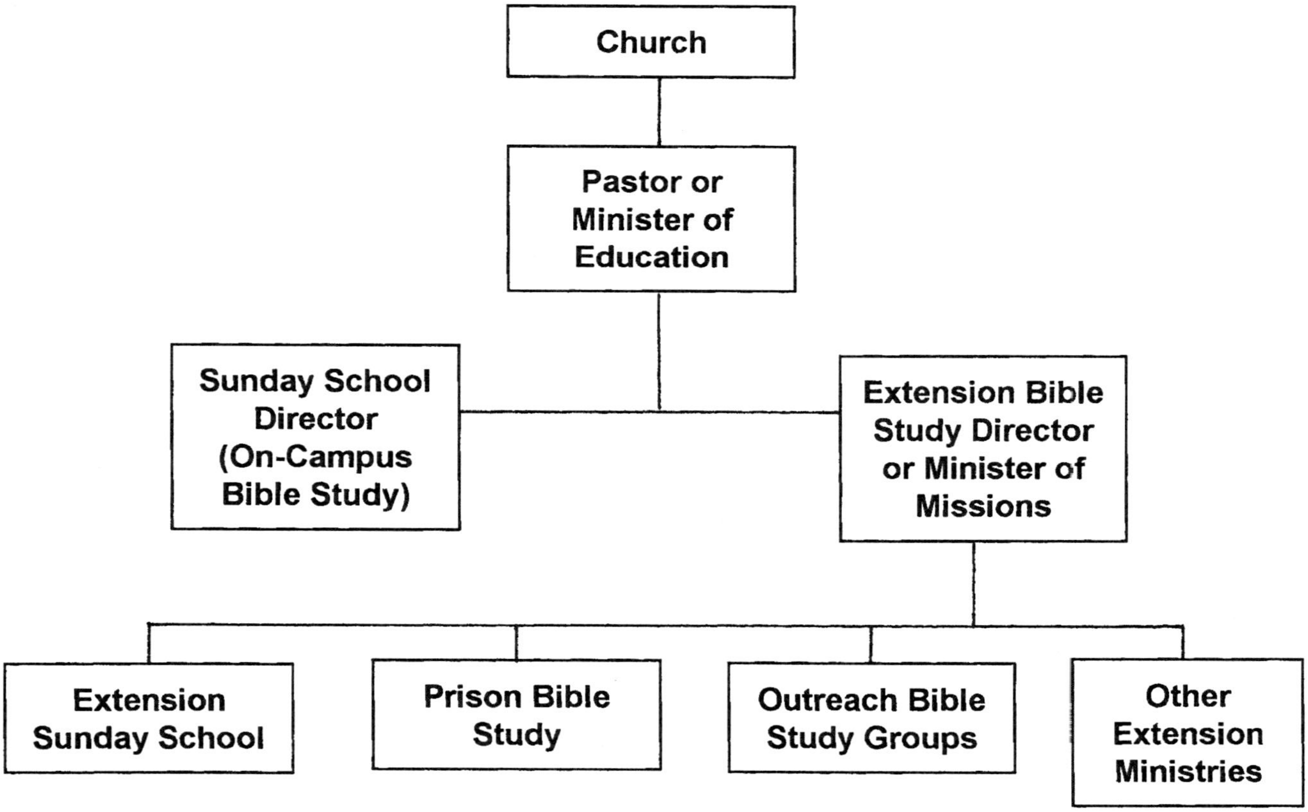

```
                    Church
                       |
              Pastor or
              Minister of
              Education
                       |
    ┌──────────────────┴──────────────────┐
 Sunday School                      Extension Bible
   Director                         Study Director
 (On-Campus                         or Minister of
 Bible Study)                          Missions
                                         |
    ┌──────────────┬──────────────┬──────────────┐
 Extension      Prison Bible   Outreach Bible     Other
 Sunday School     Study       Study Groups     Extension
                                                Ministries
```

***Organization and Structure*** – Many have criticized these approaches as being uncontrollable and unaccountable. However, unless the pastor has the habit of sitting in on adult Sunday School classes to check the teacher for doctrinal integrity, there's not a great deal of difference between on-campus and off-campus approaches. Planning and coordination are needed, and someone needs to be in charge of these ministries. Consider Figure 11 on the previous page as a possible organization for a "beginning" program.

As the number of off-campus teaching units increases and as multiple approaches are used, it is likely that additional coordinators will be needed, such as an extension Sunday School Director or an Apartment Ministry Coordinator.

What should be the purpose of these ministries? Are they spiritual half-way houses, eventually directing persons into the main on-campus ministries? Could they possibly result in a mission congregation or a new work? Or would they be perpetually dependent groups? Perhaps the best plan would be simply to begin and see where God takes your exciting new ministries.

## *Notes*

# *Endnotes*

1. Charles A. Tidwell,. *Educational Ministry of a Church.* (Nashville: Broadman Press, 1982), p. 249.

2. The information in the chart is adapted from Harry Piland and Ernest Adams, *Breakthrough: Sunday School Work.* (Nashville: Convention Press, 1990), pp. 56-58.

3. Mission Arlington, a ministry of First Baptist Church of Arlington, Texas. Tillie Burgin, Director. http://www.missionarlington.org/Multihousing.htm

4. The term "medium security" is based on the demeanor of the inmate and his potential for violence rather than the actual crime committed. Some medium security inmates may have committed acts of violence such as rape or murder. (Capital murder or death row inmates are found only in maximum security facilities.) In most instances, minimum and medium security facilities afford the greatest opportunity for inmates to gather in groups.

5. From a conversation with Rev. Charles Davenport, Pastor, First Baptist Church, Tulia, Texas, on February 21, 2001.

6. Information concerning making contact to start a prison ministry, or to find a correctional center near you.

7. Saddleback Valley Community Church in southern California was started in 1980 in the home of Pastor Rick Warren. The church grew through the multiplication of Bible study cell groups and currently averages over 10,000 in worship attendance each week. For more information about the Saddleback church or the ministry approach of its pastor and staff, see Rick Warren, *The Purpose Driven Church.* (Grand Rapids: Zondervan Publishing House), 1995.

8. This writer has discovered that youth drop out of high school for a variety of reasons, many having nothing to do with drugs, gangs, or low grades. Many do so because of their dysfunctional families. A straight-A student in Oklahoma City was suspended from school for violating the attendance policy. The fact that she often had to care for her alcoholic, drug-addicted mother accounted for tardies and absences that led to the suspension. A surprising number of dropouts are highly intelligent but experience frustration related to learning style differences. Some of my own research has indicated that intellectually "gifted" students comprise one of the largest "at-risk" groups for dropping out of high school.

# Chapter 5:
## Staffing the Organization

How many balloons can you hold at one time? Let's make them the large, round ones with no strings attached. Three? Four? Let's try an experiment, at least in our minds. Pretend that I am your minister of education and that I'm trying to enlist you to teach a young adult Sunday School class. Naturally, I want you to know what you're getting into, so I plan to tell you. Every time I give you an item on your job description, I'm going to hand you a balloon to represent that task. Are you ready? Here's what I'd like to ask you to do.

- I'd like to ask you to teach the young married adult class every Sunday morning at 9:30. *I give you the first balloon.*

- To help you with this responsibility, I'd like to ask you to attend a teachers' meeting every Wednesday evening from 6:00-7:00. *I give you another balloon.*

- You will be responsible for compiling a list of prospects for your class, visiting them regularly, and enlisting others in the class to visit. *Another balloon.*

- You will also need to contact your absentees each week. We don't want anyone slipping out the "back door." *Another balloon. I believe this makes four now.*

- A number of ministry needs will emerge from these contacts, so you will need to visit the sick and those in the hospital and prepare meals as needed. *Balloon number five.*

> *How many "balloons" are Sunday School teachers in your church trying to hold on to?*

Actually, we probably wouldn't even get to number five. The balloons would be all over the floor by this time. And I would still be waiting to give you balloons representing fellowship, prayer ministry, and records. All of these jobs need to be done, but they obviously can't be done by one person. Here's the solution: *Design, enlist, and equip a team to get the job done.* In this chapter we'll examine the design and staffing of leadership teams. In the next chapter, we'll examine ways to help that team come together and bond through training and planning.

## Designing leadership teams

In designing leadership teams, the best place to begin is with the job to be done. Review the tasks and strategies of the Sunday School from Chapter 1. Consider the things to be done within your own Sunday School. It is likely that your list could look something like this.

**Figure 12**
**Task Check List**

| Task | Class Team | Department Team |
|---|---|---|
| Administration and planning | ✔ | ✔ |
| Outreach and evangelism | ✔ | ✔ |
| Fellowship |  | ✔ |
| Teaching | ✔ |  |
| Ministry to members and non-members | ✔ |  |
| Assimilation of new members | ✔ |  |
| Prayer ministry | ✔ | ✔ |
| Family ministry | ✔ | ✔ |
| Records |  | ✔ |

In churches using the department-type organization, some of the tasks could best be carried out by the department leadership team. Recommended tasks for that team are indicated above. Some would, because of the nature of the small group, best be carried out within the class. Those are indicated above as well. The assignment of these tasks to the class team or department team could vary from one church to another.

*Should other tasks be included for your church? If so, how should those tasks be assigned?*

Figure 13 on the next page shows the organization of a department-type Sunday School and includes the organization within an adult class.

## Figure 13
## Sunday School Organization with Adult Close-up – Department Model

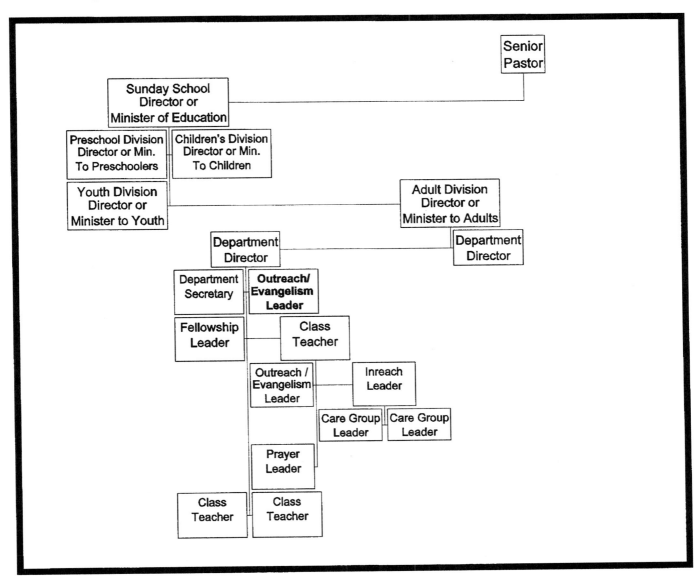

**The Sunday School Leadership Team –** Figure 14 represents the central planning group for the Sunday School. This leadership team may in some churches include the department directors. In smaller churches (class-type organization), the leadership team should include all teachers as well. Responsibilities of this team include:

- Planning, coordinating, and evaluating the total work of the Sunday School

**Figure 14**
**Sunday School Leadership Team**

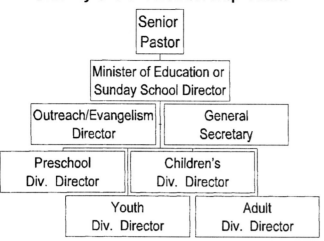

- Recommending a curriculum plan for the Sunday School; evaluating curriculum
- Recommending a budget for the Sunday School based on input from the divisions
- Coordinating the use and assignment of facilities for maximum benefit
- Determining the need for leadership; leading in the enlistment and training of those leaders
- Planning and conducting Sunday School-wide strategies for outreach, evangelism, and ministry
- Planning and coordinating the weekly officers' and teachers' meeting

**The Pastor.--** The pastor has a significant role in the leadership of the Sunday School regardless of the size of church. In the smaller church, he may be the "hands-on" leader. If this is the case, it would be essential as a first priority that he enlist and develop (disciple) a strong lay Sunday School director. The pastor and Sunday School director would then work together to enlist and train workers, plan with them on a weekly basis, and lead their efforts in outreach, evangelism, and ministry. In churches without a minister of education, the pastor would take on many of those duties as well.

The pastor of the larger, multi-staff church, would take on a different role with the Sunday School, but a very significant one. He would magnify the role of Bible study within the congregation and find every opportunity to promote the work of the Sunday School. He would encourage new members to be part of the work. He would help provide the challenge and motivation for the Sunday School to function at its best. Further, he would help to enlist a ministry staff with the expertise to give hands-on leadership to the tasks of organizing for growth, for reaching, for evangelizing, for planning, and for enlisting and training leadership. Unless the pastor happened to be a skilled religious educator by virtue of training or experience, he would probably want to delegate the leadership of the educational staff to the minister of education.

**The Minister of Education.--** The minister of education generally has primary responsibility for the leadership of the Sunday School. In most instances, he functions as a Sunday School director, serving as head of the Sunday School leadership team. If the pastor's role with the Sunday School can be described as *chief executive officer*, the role of the minister of education on the leadership is *chief operations officer*. As such, he gives leadership and supervision to others on this team, including the educational staff. Together, the leadership team carries out the list of functions beginning on page 71.

In my first staff experience as a full-time minister of education, I worked with a youth minister who reported directly to the pastor. We had overlapping responsibilities. I was responsible for leadership of all the Sunday School, including the youth division. He was responsible for all the youth ministry including the youth Sunday School. When the youth minister went to the pastor with questions related to the direction of the youth Sunday School, the pastor was able to provide little assistance. The youth minister was generally referred to me. This left the two of us with two options: Either we could lead our workers separately and in essence have two Sunday Schools (or more, depending on the number of educational staff members), or we could cooperate voluntarily. We chose the latter. When the youth minister was called from that church to serve in another church, he recommended to the pastor that his successor be placed under the supervision of the minister of education. He felt that his successor could do his best work in education under the leadership of a staff member who was equipped to provide the support he needed. Let's look briefly at the responsibilities of those on the Sunday School Leadership Team.

> *Educational staff members can do their best work under the leadership of the person who knows their work best. Generally, that would be the minister of education.*

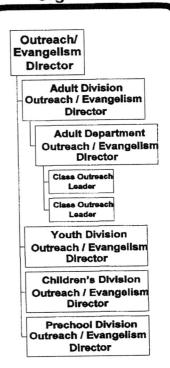

**Figure 15
Outreach/Evangelism Organization**

**The Sunday School Director.--** In churches without a minister of education, it is generally the responsibility of the Sunday School director to give guidance to the leadership team. He should work in close partnership with the pastor in assigning responsibilities to other members of the team. Specifically, the Sunday School director should:

- Meet regularly with and give leadership to the Sunday School Leadership Team as it carries out its work
- Lead in the development of an effective, flexible organization, capable of growth
- Lead in the process of enlisting and developing new leaders
- Lead the process of evaluating needs related to space, curriculum, and supplies; recommend a budget to provide for those needs
- Promote Bible study throughout the church[1]

**The Outreach/Evangelism Director.--** The outreach/ evangelism director is a specialized member of the Sunday School Leadership Team and has direct responsibility over those areas involving outreach and evangelism. Figure 15 suggests that outreach/evangelism director gives leadership to outreach/evangelism leaders throughout the Sunday School including those serving in divisions, departments, and classes. He meets with those leaders periodically to plan outreach and evangelism activities, to share and update prospect information, and to evaluate the entire process of reaching and winning people. In some churches, he also serves as the FAITH Evangelism Director, and he works with the pastor to enlist and train FAITH teams.

**Figure 16**
**The Adult Leadership Team**

```
Minister of Education
Or Sunday School Director
            |
      Adult Division
      Director or
      Minister to Adults
            |
Divisional Outreach /
Evangelism Director
            |
   ---------+---------
   |        |        |
Adult 1   Adult 2   Adult 3
Department Department Department
Director  Director  Director
```

**The Sunday School Secretary.--** In larger churches, this individual could hold a paid secretarial position. The general secretary, as this person is sometimes called, maintains enrollment and attendance records for the Sunday School and provides attendance forms for divisional and departmental secretaries throughout the Sunday School. Unless the responsibility is assigned to another person, the general secretary also maintains a file of prospects for the Sunday School and works with the outreach/evangelism director to make that information available for assignment purposes. The general secretary should meet periodically with divisional and departmental secretaries to improve the effectiveness of the record keeping system.

**Adult Leadership Team (Adult Division)** – Normally, the adult division consists of those eighteen or above, or who are married. Very large churches could have divisions for single, young, median, and senior adults. A division normally consists of two or more departments within a specified age grouping.

The adult division is normally led by a division director who reports to the Sunday School director or minister of education. It is not unusual for educational staff with age-level Sunday School responsibilities to serve in this capacity under the leadership of the minister of education. Other age-divisional leadership teams could be headed by the appropriate educational staff member. For example, the youth division Sunday

School leadership team could be headed by the minister to youth. Responsibilities of a divisional leadership team include:

- Planning and coordinating the work of the Sunday School division

- Working with general Sunday School leadership in planning and coordinating all events and on-going strategies related to their division, including leadership training, outreach/evangelism, and weekly workers' meetings

- Assisting the nominating committee or other Sunday School leadership in enlisting workers for the division

- Making recommendations for the organization of new teaching units to facilitate growth

- Evaluating all aspects of the work of the division, including teaching, curriculum, outreach, and ministry

**Figure 17**
**Adult Department Team**

```
                    ┌─ Outreach/
                    │  Evangelism ──── Class Teacher
                    │  Director
                    │
Adult Department ───┼─ Fellowship Leader ──── Class Teacher
Director            │
                    │
                    └─ Department ──── Class Teacher
                       Secretary
```

**The Adult Department Leadership Team.**-- Membership of this team might vary from church to church. We've included the director, secretary, outreach-evangelism leader, fellowship leader, and teachers. The primary function of this team is to coordinate the teaching, outreach, evangelism, ministry, and fellowship that would go on within the adult department. Specific responsibilities are as follows:

- **Director** – Gives leadership to the adult department team, leads the weekly departmental planning meeting, assists in enlistment and orientation of teachers and other team members, and helps to evaluate the work of the department.

- **Outreach/Evangelism Director** – Serves on the church's outreach/evangelism team. Works with the Sunday School outreach/evangelism director and class outreach leaders in promoting outreach, providing information on prospects, and training people to make evangelistic and ministry visits.

- **Fellowship Leader** – Coordinates the planning and promotion of fellowship activities, seeks ways to help each member and prospect feel accepted and be involved, and supports the work of class fellowship leaders or inreach leaders.

- **Department Secretary** – Works within the church's record keeping system to keep and update records for enrollment, attendance, new members, and guests. It is recommended that one department secretary maintain attendance records for each of the classes to make greater use of limited teaching time in the small groups.

**Departmental Leadership Teams in Other Divisions** – Preschool and children's departments normally use a much simpler structure. In most instances, the leadership team consists of the director, a sufficient number of teachers to maintain a proper teacher-pupil ratio, and a department secretary. If preschool or children's departments within their respective divisions are located in the same area of the building, their records could be maintained by a divisional secretary. In many instances, the outreach/evangelism director for the division would serve the needs of the departments within that division. The organization of youth departments is similar to the organizations in the adult departments.

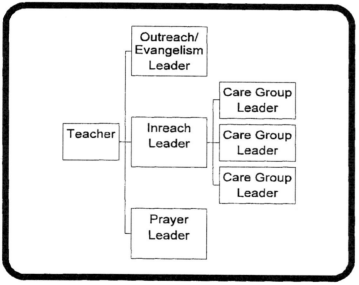

**Figure 18**
**Class Leadership Team**

**Class Leadership Teams** – If a church is to grow and reach people through the Sunday School, the success of that venture will be dependent to a large degree on the health and effectiveness of the adult Sunday School class. Adult Sunday School classes have the potential to . . .

- ☐ Accept and assimilate guests, new members, and new Christians, *or* keep them at arm's length and essentially reject them.

- ☐ Teach transformational truths of the Bible, *or* perpetuate an impotent "cultural" brand of Christianity.

- ☐ Permit and foster growth through aggressive outreach and evangelism, *or* retard that growth through a traditional mind-set that places the class above the church and its mission.

- ☐ Keep members involved and active through consistent ministry *or* allow them to slip away through the back door through apathy.

- ☐ Generate potential teachers and leaders for other classes and ministries of the church *or* hold on to those members by valuing their class loyalty more than their service to Christ.

- ☐ Equip Christian parents to provide godly leadership in their homes *or* ignore their needs assuming that Christian families don't have problems and that Christian parents don't need help.

> *How many "positives" do you recognize in the Sunday School classes in your church? How many "negatives?"*

- ☐ Equip believers to understand and exercise their spiritual gifts through selfless service to Christ in the church and community, *or* perpetuate the idea that service is "what we pay the preacher to do."

No other organizational entity in the church has as much potential to permit or forbid successful evangelistic growth and ministry as the adult class. Many adult classes are still following the old traditional models, however. As I lead adult Sunday School conferences, I am often asked about the duties of class officers. I usually begin by mentioning the things I'm about to list. *No,* they reply. *What about the class President, the Vice-President, the Treasurer, and the Membership Chairman?* My response is that they no longer exist. In seeker-friendly small group Bible study classes committed to reach, teach, evangelize, and minister to a wide range of people, they simply have little or no place.

Perhaps the best way of examining the function of the adult class leadership team is to examine the responsibilities of the following team members:

- **Teacher –**

    1. Give leadership to the class team, and participate as a member of the department leadership team.

    2. Pray regularly for each member and prospect and for the ability to address their needs through the presentation of the lesson.

    3. Prepare and conduct the weekly Bible study experience using appropriate curriculum materials and methods.

4. Meet with other teachers and department leaders for weekly planning.

5. Participate in, and encourage learners to participate in, outreach and evangelism efforts.

6. Seek to grow through participation in regular training events.

- **Outreach/Evangelism Leader –**

    1. Participate as a member of the Class Leadership Team and the Sunday School Outreach Team.

    2. Work with department outreach director to provide names of prospects for visitation by class members or evangelism teams.

    3. Participate in, and encourage class members to participate in, regular outreach and evangelism activities.

    4. Encourage class members to receive training in outreach and personal evangelism.

    5. Seek to grow through participation in appropriate training activities.

- **Prayer Leader -**

    1. Work with inreach leader and other class members to determine prayer needs of members and prospects; share prayer concerns with members.

    2. Serve as a liaison between the class and the church's prayer ministry.

    3. Inform class members of nature and purpose of the church's prayer ministry; seek to enlist participants in that ministry.

    4. Participate in regular outreach and evangelism activities.

    5. Seek to grow through participation in appropriate training activities.

- **Inreach Leader -**

    1. Participate as a member of the class leadership team.

2. Enlist and give leadership to care group leaders; maintain a ratio of one care group leader for every 5 to 7 members and prospects.

3. Assign new Christians in the class to a care group leader or member who can disciple and encourage them.

4. Assign all class members, leaders, and guests to a care group leader. (Even care group leaders should be part of someone else's care group).

5. Participate in, and encourage group leaders to participate in, regular outreach and evangelism activities.

6. Seek to grow through participation in appropriate training activities.

- **Care Group Leaders -**

    1. Participate as a member of the class leadership team.

    2. Accept an assignment of 5-7 members and prospects to contact regularly.

    3. Contact members of care group regularly, particularly when absences occur.

    4. Report ministry needs to the class; seek to involve others in helping to meet those needs.

    5. Participate in regular outreach and evangelism activities.

    6. Seek to grow through participation in appropriate training activities.

- **Class Members –**

    1. Make personal spiritual and study preparation for Bible study each week.

    2. Seek to apply biblical truths to daily life and make them part of family worship.

    3. Seek to develop a personal ministry.

    4. Participate in regular outreach and evangelism activities.

5. Give names of friends, relatives, neighbors, and others who are not involved in regular Bible study to the class outreach leader for assignment; seek to invite these individuals to participate.

6. Allow Bible study to result in personal spiritual transformation and preparation for service on the front lines of the community and the world.

**A Word About Youth Classes** – Many have discovered that youth classes can benefit from an organization similar to that in the adult class. At the very least, every youth class should have an outreach-evangelism leader and care group leaders. In many instances, mature youth could serve in these capacities.

## Leadership teams for small churches

If yours is a smaller church, one organized around classes rather than departments, you may be wondering about the benefits of the organization described above for your ministry. While it is true that your church could do without some of the leaders and teams listed above, it is untrue that organization is unnecessary. How much organization is enough for the smaller church?

Review the Sunday School Organization Chart (Figure 9, page 60). Note these elements of organization.

> *Many smaller churches get by with a Sunday School director and an inadequate number of teachers. Is yours one of those?*

**General Planning Team** – The pastor, Sunday School director, outreach-evangelism director, and perhaps the secretary need to meet regularly to provide overall leadership for the Sunday School.

**The Role of Division Directors** – Almost every smaller church has the four natural age divisions: Preschool, Children, Youth, and Adult. It would be extremely helpful to appoint division directors to work with teachers in their age divisions. Since no departments directors are involved, division directors should provide direct leadership of teachers by planning with them, helping to meet their needs, and providing encouragement to participate in schedule outreach and training events. Division directors could also assist with record keeping, literature ordering and distribution, and maintaining and sharing prospect information.

**The Class Leadership Team** – Adult and youth classes in the small church differ very little from those in larger churches. Adult and youth classes should have an outreach/evangelism leader, an appropriate number of care group leaders, and possibly even an inreach leader. In every instance, their duties would be basically the same as for those in the larger churches.

## *Staffing leadership teams*

A natural thought at this point is *Where will my church get all the workers to staff the positions described above?* The simple answer to that question is that God provides every church with the human resources necessary to carry out His will. That concept is seen in 1 Corinthians 12. In this chapter, Paul describes the way believers are uniquely gifted to help the church carry out its work. Paul stresses the complementary nature of members' individual gifts as well as their mutual dependence. In Ephesians 4, Paul adds that the members of Christ's body must equipped by pastors and teachers to *do the work of ministry so that the body of Christ might be built up (Eph. 4:10-11, CSB).* Consider these principles as you approach the task of staffing:

- Begin with the belief that Christian service is a normative, not an optional, activity reserved for the extremely committed
- Consider the gifts, talents, interests, and *passions* of every member, including new members.
- Develop a framework of policies for workers.
- Base enlistment strategies on the ministry to be carried out, not the needs within the organization.
- Use good enlistment procedures.

**Service: The Normal Christian Life** – One of the key differences between successful and unsuccessful churches rests in what members of the church expect of themselves and of each other. The mind-set in every church ought to be that service for the Christian is not only desirable, it is expected. A point of beginning in this process is with prospective members. It is only fair to let them know that yours is a church which expects every member to serve according to his spiritual gifts and God-given talents and passions. A more difficult task will be showing long-term members that service is not an option for them either. In a day when many couples join a church based on what that church has to offer them, this may sound like poor advice. Yet it works.

> *Have you ever heard it said, "I don't need to serve because I don't need to pay for my salvation"?*

**Consider Gifts, Talents, Interests, and *Passions*** – The foundational training that is available to every member should include opportunities for believers to become aware of their spiritual giftedness and to be trained according to those gifts. More will be said about this type of training in the next chapter.

Develop a talent and interest survey form to give to every member over a period of several weeks, then on an on-going basis to every new member that joins. Ask members to indicate their interest, experience, and degree of expertise in a wide variety of ministries. In the survey, include a few questions seeking information related to language skills, blood type, cross-cultural experience, and certifications in health or education fields. Part of the reason for this will become more apparent in the ***Blended ministry*** section of this chapter. Compile the information and feed it into a computer data base in the church office. This information should be made available to leaders who are charged with seeking new workers. Its availability will virtually eliminate the possibility that people will be overlooked and will discourage the practice of assigning too many jobs to one individual.

**What Should the Church Expect of Workers?** – Generally, every person who serves in a leadership capacity should be a born-again believer and a faithful member of the church. Beyond this, every church should develop its own set of policies and expectations. Consider these:

- Active involvement in an adult Sunday School class (for those not currently in a leadership position)
- An exemplary Christian lifestyle at home, in the community, in the workplace, and at church, including freedom from use of alcohol, tobacco, and non-prescription drugs
- Willingness to be trained in the duties of the responsibility for which they are being enlisted
- Willingness to be involved in the church's ministries of outreach and evangelism
- Willingness to take this responsibility as a major (if not exclusive) commitment; willingness to divest themselves of activities as needed to make the required level of commitment possible
- Faithfulness in attendance
- Loyalty to the church and its leadership
- Willingness to submit to a screening process if the assignment involves preschoolers, children, or youth

**A Workers' Covenant?** – This is for each church to decide. In a covenant, those agreeing to serve as Sunday School workers make a formal, signed commitment to adhere to the standards of that covenant. In developing your covenant, consider the list above as a starting point. Could or should these be formalized? Would the covenant accomplish the purpose of helping Sunday School workers be more committed to their tasks, or would it have a detrimental effect? This is an issue for each church to decide.

**Security issues in enlistment.--** Paul wrote, *But among you there should not even be a hint of sexual immorality* (Eph. 5:3, HCSB). The nature of the society in which we live demands that churches exercise extreme caution in enlisting workers with preschoolers, children, or youth. These procedures may seem distasteful or even insulting to some; they are nevertheless necessary. Develop the practice of screening everyone, beginning with staff, and seek to convey the following purpose of screening: to minimize risk of sexual and other forms of abuse to children and to safeguard the reputation and witness of your church. This process should seek to confirm the identity of everyone who works with children and should fulfill all local legal requirements.[2]

**Take a Ministry-Based Approach** – All too frequently, ministers of education or other leaders responsible for enlistment begin to panic around the first of August when there is an uncomfortably large number of vacancies in the Sunday School organizational chart. The tendency is to start plugging these holes with anyone who is willing. I'm sorry to say that *I've been there, done that, and have the t-shirt.* I've talked with a large number of workers who were "coerced" into taking a class for a short time *"until we can find a permanent teacher,"* and that may have been 20 years ago. The organizational chart can live for a while without having every hole filled. Resist the temptation to panic. The end result of this type of enlistment is an organization filled with people who are only marginally committed. There's a better way.

Ministry-based enlistment begins with the needs of the potential worker, not the needs of the organization. Every believer needs to serve. Every believer has a spiritual gift which needs to be exercised. Every believer has a passion to do something. We must also begin with the needs of the ministry to be carried out. Remember that *God provides every church with the human resources necessary to carry out His will.* When churches magnify Christ and the ministries into which He is leading them, He will burden His people throughout the congregation, preparing them to serve. If necessary, He will send people to you who are not even members of your church at the present time.

**Understand the Reasons for Difficulties in Enlistment** – Some churches find it difficult if not impossible to find workers for all the needs in the Sunday School and other church programs and ministries. A few others have a backlog of potential workers ready to step in when a vacancy occurs or a new position is created. It's possible for *both* of these conditions to exist within the same church. Why? Figure 19 on the next page should provide some insight into enlistment-related difficulties.

## Figure 19
## How Difficult is Enlistment in Your Church?

| Churches will have *difficulty* enlisting workers if these conditions exist: | Churches will have *little difficulty* enlisting workers if these conditions exist |
|---|---|
| 1. Sense of boredom<br>2. No real awareness of the church's mission<br>3. No opportunity for workers to contribute to the planning and shaping of ministries; everything is planned and directed by the pastor or staff<br>4. Low level of expectation of worker performance (anyone can do this job)<br>5. Too few people in the church doing too many jobs<br>6. Lack of healthy communication between staff and laity | 1. Spirit of enthusiasm and expectancy<br>2. Belief in and commitment to the church's mission<br>3. Opportunities for workers to contribute to the planning and shaping of ministries<br>4. High level of expectation of worker performance (this requires real commitment)<br>5. Many people in the church taking on focused responsibilities<br>6. High degree of healthy communication between staff and laity |

**Use a Good Enlistment Procedure** – The nominating committee is normally the group within the church charged with enlistment of Sunday School leaders and leadership for other ministries. To be effective, the nominating committee needs knowledge of several areas of church life. *First*, they need to be aware of the present and future ministry directions. *Second*, this group needs to have a broad base of knowledge of the church membership. *Third*, the nominating committee needs a working understanding of the Sunday School, its leadership teams, and the kinds of leaders who are needed.

> *How many of the conditions mentioned in the left column of Figure 19 exist in your church?*

It would be virtually impossible for a church-elected committee to possess all the knowledge or information needed to do an effective job. Guidance and input will be needed from at least two *human* sources. The pastor, minister of education, and other trained educational staff members must be available to provide leadership related to ministry direction and organizational expansion. Further, key age-level Sunday School leaders must be available to help interpret the needs in every area. The following criteria should be considered in selecting members for this committee.

- Members should be prayerful, continually seeking God's direction, and putting His "gentle nudges" over human instinct and wisdom.
- Members should be willing and able to maintain confidentiality.

- Members of this committee should themselves be committed workers in church ministries.
- Members must be willing to deal with sensitive and at times difficult issues.
- Members must be willing to learn anything they need to know about the work of the Sunday School.

## Figure 20
## A Procedure for Selecting Sunday School Workers

1. **Determine needs for workers**
   - Consider new ministry directions or programs such as extension Bible study ministries
   - Determine growth of organization. How many new classes or departments will be needed
   - Consider development within organization. Are you adding outreach/evangelism leaders? Inreach leaders? Others?
   - Consider resignations of existing workers or other needs to replace existing workers

2. **Develop a master list of potential workers**
   - From talent and interest surveys
   - From spiritual gift inventories
   - From adult Sunday School teachers
   - From personal knowledge of the congregation. Do not, however, rely too heavily on personal knowledge, thus overlooking potential workers you might not know
   - From potential worker training courses and/or spiritual formations courses.

3. **Do preliminary screening**
   - From the master list, determine those who meet the general qualifications determined earlier.
   - Ask, *If this person were available and willing, would he/she be the type of individual we would want to serve?* This question goes beyond the previous one to raise issues such as personality, human relations skills, personal appearance, and hygiene.

4. **Break the resulting list down into basic personality types and age-group interests**
   - Most people have strengths in one of these three basic areas: in teaching, in organization and administration, or in people-skills. Use interest surveys and spiritual gifts information to list people in one of these three areas.
   - Re-group the list based on these categories for consideration as potential teachers, directors, or outreach leaders.

*Continued from the previous page*

5. **Begin to prayerfully make match-ups between needs and potential workers**
   - Begin at the top of the organization and work down: Sunday School general officers, divisional leadership, department directors, teachers, and departmental officers.
   - Be especially sensitive to the leadership of the Holy Spirit in this process, but listen also to staff and divisional leadership.

6. **Determine the *where* and *who* of enlistment**
   - Make the contact by appointment, and arrange a time and place convenient to all parties, one which is free from distractions, and one which would allow ample opportunity to visit.
   - The nominating committee might not be the best group to make the contact. Ideally, Sunday School workers should be enlisted by the person serving as their team leader. (For example, a teacher would be enlisted by a department director.) Consider a staff member or nominating committee member going with the appropriate team leader.

7. **Consider the *content* of the visit**
   - Pray before making the visit – not for a "yes," but for God's leadership to be felt.
   - Bring necessary materials: Sunday School curriculum, a list of other members on the team, and a written job description.
   - Discuss "generals" before discussing "specifics." Talk about the nature of the commitment and its importance. Introduce the concept of Workers' Covenant at this point if you use this tool.
   - Discuss the specific requirements of the job. Don't try to overwhelm the potential worker, but at the same time be honest about the expectations. If you want this worker to attend Wednesday night teachers' meetings, now is the time to bring that up. Include other appropriate expectations such as participation in outreach and training events.
   - Explore the curriculum.
   - Answer questions honestly.
   - If a preschool, children, or youth worker is being considered, seek permission for a background check.
   - Make information available related to necessary training events.
   - Be sure that if a "yes" answer is being considered, the priorities of God first, family second, church responsibilities third will not be violated.
   - Agree on a time frame for the decision and a time and place to meet.
   - Pray with the potential worker.

*Continued from the previous page*

8. **Respect the answer, even if it is "no."**
   - Try to learn why a "no" is a "no." Perhaps another place of service could be considered, or perhaps the time is not right for now.
   - Above all, never try to talk the individual into a "yes" response. *(Hint: This is probably a reason why the pastor should not make enlistment visits. Many members would be reluctant to say "no" to a pastor, even if the answer should be "no."*

9. **Conduct the necessary background check.**

10. **Depending on the response of the candidate or the results of the background check, either**
    - Go back to Step 5 and repeat the enlistment process or
    - Recommend the willing worker to the church for election.

# Blended ministry

The first eighteen pages of this chapter have dealt with the design and staffing of traditional leadership teams – those that exist on-campus. What about off-campus ministries?

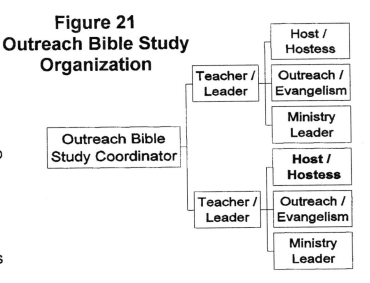

**Figure 21
Outreach Bible Study Organization**

Very little has ever been written on principles for structuring and staffing leadership teams for the wide variety of off-campus Bible study ministries. Principles that guide the more traditional organizations might or might not be appropriate in non-traditional settings. That leaves two possibilities: *adapt* or *invent*. Actually, some of the more traditional principles should work well in off-campus settings. An optimum size for a Bible study class, for example, would be fairly consistent. The organization for a traditional adult Sunday School class would need to be adapted to the needs of an apartment-based Bible study cell group, however. In some instances the off-campus organization would be very different from the more traditional version. Those involved in these ministries would literally learn as they go, with God providing the on-the-job training. *Invent,* in this context, means allowing God to take you to places you never dreamed of going to do things you never imagined yourself doing.

With this in mind, let's begin with some things we know. First, extension Bible study units, wherever they exist, must always be accountable to the church. Lines of communication must be open in both directions. The organizational structure needs to provide for that. Review Figure 11, page 66, and determine how this structure should be modified to fit your situation. For example, if a number of outreach Bible study groups existed in dozens of separate locations, an outreach Bible study director would be needed. If the prison Bible study were part of a larger prison ministry, someone would need to guide that ministry as well. Let's briefly look at some specific examples:

**Extension Sunday School** – An extension Sunday School functions organizationally much like a traditional on-campus Sunday School. Both need general leadership and a staff of teachers. The simplified small-church organizational model should be appropriate for the extension Sunday School. The leadership team should consist of the director, the outreach/evangelism director, and divisional leaders.

**Outreach Bible Study** – Let's assume that you are working with a network of outreach Bible study classes meeting primarily in apartments complexes and mobile homes. Briefly, the outreach Bible study coordinator would coordinate the ministries at the various locations, secure new locations, and help enlist and train workers for the sites. He or she would work under the leadership of the minster of education, minister of missions, or another assigned staff member. The teacher/leader would focus on Bible study and leadership of the site team. The host or hostess would be responsible for the physical location, refreshments, furniture and equipment, and welcoming participants. The outreach/evangelism leader would be responsible for involving members in reaching others and in sharing the gospel with non-believers. The ministry leader would seek to discover ministry needs and address those needs through the involvement of the class and the ministry resources of the church.

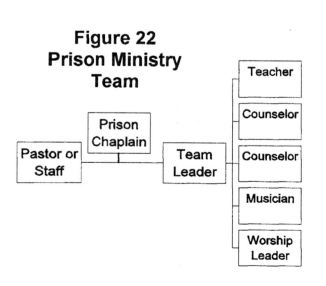

**Figure 22 Prison Ministry Team**

**Prison Ministry** – The membership of a prison ministry team depends on the type of ministry being conducted. In many instances, Bible study is limited to a single class, even though that class could be quite large. This is primarily due to the limitation of facilities. Most prisons are limited to a single room for "educational" purposes. The leader of the prison ministry team must report to two individuals: the pastor (or assigned staff member or extension ministry leader) of the church and the chaplain of the prison. The relationship between the team leader and the chaplain cannot be overemphasized. Rules must be strictly followed to ensure the safety of the ministry team as well as the inmates and prison staff. Failure to do so will almost certainly result in loss of visitation and ministry privileges.

**City Church, Amarillo, Texas –** Many people thought Pastor Don Lane's idea was so far out in left field they wouldn't touch it. Very little financial assistance came from denominational church planting resources because it was believed that Don's idea would fail. During Don's recovery process (mentioned in the introduction to Part 2), God gave him his "unusual" ideas about church planting. He began to listen.

Don knew how to grow churches. That had never been the problem. In fact, he knew how to start new churches and how to grow them from mission status to financial independence in three years. Ordinary wisdom dictated that new churches be started in new communities, or at the very least in communities that were growing and attracting white, middle-class baby-boomers. While Don saw absolutely nothing wrong with attracting baby-boomers and winning them to Christ, he felt that Amarillo didn't need any more white, middle-class churches. He felt that a much larger group of people was being neglected.

Over a period of time, God taught Don Lane how He wanted him to start churches: by doing the opposite of what everyone else was doing. The result was City Church in Amarillo, Texas. From the very beginning, City Church was designed to reach the people that no one else wanted. "Go to the worst first" became the motto of this new endeavor.

> *Could you make a list of communities in your city or region that are essentially unreached because the more affluent churches have moved out?*

One of the first difficult lessons Don learned was to start with those who could be reached – children first, then youth. Missions-minded adults became interested in this ministry and joined to help. Don's people taught them, loved them, led them to Christ, and in many ways became for them their Christian parents. The church helped the children pay for band instruments, sent them on field trips, and took care of many of their clothing needs. The attendance was growing so rapidly with children and youth that the church had literally run out of workers. Don had to go to his adults and tell them that their classes were temporarily being discontinued because they were all needed to work with children. More will be said about this ministry in later chapters.[3]

In organizing the City Church ministry, Don and his wife assembled a leadership team consisting of family members and several others who were specialized in various areas. The leadership team functioned as the core planning group. Members of this team then enlisted volunteers in their areas of responsibility to carry out specific tasks. Once assigned, these tasks were the domain of that particular volunteer. Don used the kitchen supervisor as an example. "That's her area. In the kitchen, she tells *me* what to do, not the other way around." Don puts teenagers who have grown up in the ministry over the past five or six years as interns, grooming them to accept ministry responsibilities.

**Hispanic Mission of Immanuel Baptist, Shawnee, Oklahoma–** The team approach is now an active organization strategy throughout areas of the world served by missionaries of the International Mission Board. This is the concept that missionaries Mark and Mary Fuller brought to the Hispanic work in Shawnee. The church planting team is headed by the missionaries themselves. They have been trained for the job, and they have accumulated years of experience planting churches in Hispanic communities. They have assembled a team consisting of two additional couples, all skilled in Spanish and all committed to the task. This group functions as the strategy team, with the responsibility for making the basic ministry decisions. General oversight will be provided by the pastor and the missions committee of the church. *It is important that missions leadership teams, wherever they serve, have the freedom to develop their basic strategies, with only the broadest parameters provided by an administrative superstructure.*

**Adaptability, Flexibility, Accountability** – These are the three key descriptors for church-based community Bible study ministries. It is possible that your church may discover ministry opportunities where few others have gone before, and for which there are no established organizational patterns. Many of the principles and methods appropriate for traditional organizations will need to be adapted to new and challenging situations, if they are to work at all.

Flexibility is of utmost importance. In off-campus settings, ministry conditions change rapidly as new opportunities present themselves. Maintain the ministry team mind-set, but allow the composition of those teams to vary as needed. Be prepared to seek out others to join the team.

Accountability to the church is a constant that must be maintained to insure the quality of the ministry and to enable its growth. *In maintaining accountability, focus on the principles, not the methods; on the goals, not the strategies.* Much of your ministry will be done where there are no textbooks to guide and no traditions to fall back upon. If there are any "experts" at all, it will be those actually doing the work. Provide help and support as needed, but allow the ministry teams the freedom to do what God is teaching them to do in the on-the-job training only He can provide.

## Notes

# Endnotes

1. Unless otherwise noted, the job descriptions in this chapter have been influenced by and/or adapted from Bill L. Taylor and Louis B. Hanks, *Sunday School for a New Century.* (Nashville: LifeWay Press, 1999), pp. 90-96.

2. These and other suggestions are found in Richard R. Hammar, Steven W. Klipowscz, and James F. Cobble, *Reducing the Risk of Child Sexual Abuse in Your Church.* (Matthews, NC: Christian Ministry Resources, 1993).

3. From a telephone conversation with Don Lane, Pastor, City Church, 205 S. Polk, Amarillo, Texas, on March 15, 2001.

# Chapter 6
## Becoming a Team

It was five-year old Stephen's first soccer game. His team won handily, scoring six goals. *How many of those goals did you score?* his grandfather asked. Stephen replied, *"Coach says that we're a team. When one of us scores we all score.* Stephen's coach was right. On teams, there are no "stars." Everyone is a player. When one wins, the team wins. When one is defeated, the entire team suffers that same defeat.

In the previous chapter, we examined the composition and purpose of teams and we learned some techniques for assembling the members of a team. These things do not make teams, however. Some so-called teams are in reality just collections of individuals looking out for their own self-interests and concerned with their own advancement. Such "teams" have been likened to chains that are only as strong as their weakest link. Becoming a team involves a bonding process. Through this process of bonding, we come understand and fully appreciate the other members of the team. We learn of their strengths that are complementary to ours. Members of the team energize and encourage each other. In reality, teams are nothing like chains. Genuine teams are actually stronger than the combined strength of all their individual members.

> *Chains are only as strong as their weakest links. This is not true of teams, which are actually **stronger** than the sum of their individual members.*

My own lessons in team building came in helping to assemble teams of volunteers to do mission work in Argentina. Every six months a group of 20 to 30 individuals, some of whom had not known each other previously, bonded as a team and went on an eleven-day venture into the unknown. The work these teams did was incredible. Their sense of unity and purpose was itself a witness and a testimony to the unity Christ desires for all of us. The process was not automatic. On the contrary, it required intentional effort. We spent many hours together in training, planning, praying, and even playing. On the mission field, individual team members at times experienced physical illness, stress, and disappointment. In those times of weakness, other members of the team shared their strength. We rejoiced in each other's victories. Like the members of Stephen's soccer team, *we all scored.* And so it is with Sunday School leadership teams.

## Teams bonding through training

The training of teachers and leaders in churches is rapidly becoming a lost art. Fewer and fewer churches schedule regular training classes. That fact just doesn't make sense. Public school teachers are trained and accredited to guide young minds. Auto mechanics must be trained and even certified to work on car engines. In fact, training is essential in virtually any field that can be named, apparently with one exception: *Those who teach eternally-significant biblical truths are evidently exempt.* We assume that if a Christian has had a relationship with Christ for several years and has been involved in a Sunday School class, he or she is ready to be a teacher. In reality, nothing could be further from the truth.

There was a time that teachers were trained. Discipleship Training (previously known as Church Training or Training Union) has had a long-standing tradition for training workers through study courses. In the past, numerous training opportunities were available and were well-utilized. The problem is not in the lack of opportunities because *all of these approaches are still available.* A vast array of training materials are produced each year by LifeWay Christian Resources. *The Christian Growth Study Plan*, like its predecessor, the *Church Study Course*, offers many options for personal growth and development of leadership skills.[1]

### Six Steps to Effective Leader Training

1. Develop a positive environment for training
2. Discover training needs
3. Design a training curriculum
4. Develop a training strategy
5. Maintain a high level of quality
6. Evaluate the effectiveness

What explains the lack of participation in training events in most churches? Is it that educational staff members and other would-be trainers do not know the basics of Sunday School work well enough to teach others? Is it that members and leaders are just too busy today? Is it apathy and boredom? Perhaps to one degree or another, all these things are true. Christ commissioned some to be pastors and teachers *for the training of the saints in the work of ministry, to build up the body of Christ.* (Ephesians 4:12, HCSB) *And what you have heard from me in the presence of many witnesses, commit to faithful men who will be able to teach others also.* (2 Timothy 2:2, HCSB). Paul's instructions to first-century churches are still applicable today. We just can't seem to get around the biblical necessity for teaching those who will be responsible for passing the Christian message and heritage on to the next generation.

**1** **Develop a Positive Environment for Training** – The concept is basically simple: Our work of teaching the eternal truths of the Bible to people in such a way as to lead them to make a faith commitment to Christ, to grow as believers, and to emerge as teachers and leaders who can teach the next generation is of paramount importance. It deserves the best that we can give it. The "best" requires that those who teach these eternal truths must be trained. Consider the following components of this positive environment:

- The importance of training must be seen in pastors and educational staff members who have been trained and who are committed to improvement through continuous training. This personal commitment to training must be visible for all to see.

- Pastors and educational staff members who exemplify the benefits of training may then expect the same of those they lead. While serving as a minister of education at a church in Grand Prairie, Texas, I led an educational staff that modeled training for their staff of volunteer teachers and leaders. We engaged in a personal study of the books we would be teaching. We were seen attending professional conferences for the sole purpose of continuing to grow. This had an effect as we then conveyed this expectation of training to volunteer leaders. They were willing to respond because they saw that training was important to us.

- This expectation that leaders be trained must in some way be formalized either through a workers' covenant or through the enlistment process.

> *Does your church require that its elected teachers and leaders be trained? If not, how can that position be justified?*

- Priority time must be allotted for training events, courses, and seminars. One church I know has built its Sunday evening program around training rather than worship. Following a brief worship experience starting at 5:00 PM, a full hour and a half is devoted to training at the various levels to be described in this chapter.

- Teachers and leaders must come to expect it of each other. Training must become part of the growth emphasis of your church.

**2** **Determine Training Needs** – There is no simple method for determining the training needs of workers and potential workers as every church will be unique. If you are new on a church staff, most of your first year will be required for this process. Actually, the ministry start-up period will afford the best opportunity to learn about your church, its Sunday School leadership, and their needs. Consider the following strategies:

- *Review the training history of your church.* Your purpose here is to determine what, if any, training has taken place in the five years prior to your arrival. Information that is older than that will have very little use. Visit with teachers and leaders who have served several years, with senior and support staff, and check the files and back issues of the church newsletters for information regarding training events. Include spiritual formation courses such as *Master Life* and *Experiencing God,* as well as evangelistic training which might not relate directly to the Sunday School. Put down on paper a three to five year history of these events, and begin to get a picture of areas emphasized as well as those neglected.

- *Talk with current teachers and leaders.* Visit with workers concerning areas in which they perceive the need for help. Include in this informal survey teaching methods, understanding of curriculum, understanding of age-level characteristics, Sunday School organization, and training in outreach.

- *Conduct formal surveys.* Actually, this can be one of the most effective tools as it combines benefits of the first two methods. Develop a survey form which seeks information related to participation in past events, perceived areas of need, and an indication of the best times for training.

- *Observe the present situation.* This will be an on-going activity involving the following:

    1. <u>Attendance records</u>. Does attendance start off strong at the beginning of the year, then taper off during the year? This may reveal a need for training in methodology, outreach, and ministry.

    2. <u>Ease of enlistment</u>. Is it easy or difficult to enlist workers? Difficulty in enlistment could reveal a need for training in a number of areas, including spiritual readiness. Review the chart in Figure19 on page 84.

    3. <u>Level of enthusiasm</u>. Do you hear people talking positively about Sunday School? About their role in the Sunday School? Are they telling and inviting their friends?

4. <u>Other performance areas</u>. This is the miscellaneous area which can include everything from the way curriculum is utilized to the way ministry contacts are made.

**3. Design a Training Curriculum** – The pyramid to the right illustrates three levels of training that should be considered. The foundation of the pyramid is participation in the on-going Sunday School program. *Level 1* consists of spiritual formation courses, *Level 2* involves more advanced Bible study than would normally be available on Sunday mornings, and *Level 3* would be the functional areas related to the Sunday School ministry itself.

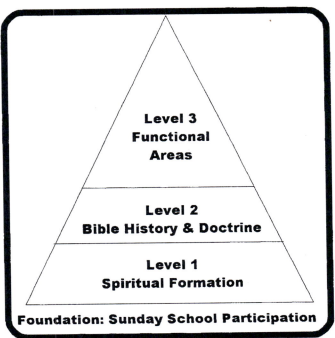

Figure 23
Training Pyramid

The common denominator for training for all workers and potential workers should be the Sunday School. Potential teachers and leaders should be the product of every adult class. Growth toward Christian maturity should occur over a period of several years. Adult teachers should be led to nurture and disciple at least one potential teacher each year.

**Level 1** should be open to all church members who are growing through regular Bible study. The *Spiritual Formation* stage should include, but not necessarily be limited to, spiritual gifts studies and courses such as *Master Life*, *Prayer Life*, *Experiencing God*, and *Fresh Encounter*. The purposes of these courses should be to heighten spiritual awareness and help deepen desires on the part of believers to live the Christ-like life. More will be said later about the scheduling of these courses.

**Level 2** should be required of all potential teachers and could be part of a teacher training program. A survey course in Old and New Testament history would be a good beginning point. Shortened versions of this course are available through the church's Discipleship Training program; more intensive studies are available through local Baptist colleges and universities and Seminary Extension. A growing number of these courses are available through Internet-based delivery

*Level 1: Spiritual Formation*
*Level 2: Bible and Doctrine*
*Level 3: Sunday School courses*

systems. The survey course provides help to teachers who may never have been exposed to Bible history and helps learners to contextualize Bible stories.

Further, we live in a time when many members will move in and out of churches based on reasons other than doctrine. Within any congregation there is much diversity on a variety of doctrinal issues. Even though many Baptist churches baptize new members who come in from other denominations, that act of baptism does nothing to address doctrinal concerns. Courses such as *The Baptist Faith and Message* or *Doctrines Baptists Believe* could prove helpful. A final component of Level 2 should include a short course in principles of biblical interpretation.

**Level 3** is most directly related to the Sunday School. Whereas courses in Levels 1 and 2 are foundational in nature and would be appropriate for any Christian, Level 3 courses have a practical application for current and potential Sunday School teachers and leaders. At this third level, consider courses or training topics such as:

1. Sunday School organization and administration
2. Principles of teaching and learning
3. Effective teaching methods
4. Outreach and evangelism
5. Understanding and use of curriculum materials
6. Understanding of age level characteristics

**4 Develop a Training Strategy**– The best approaches to leader training may be summed up in a single word: *Variety*. Despite your best efforts, workers will not be able to attend every training workshop you conduct. By varying the time, format, and location of training, everyone should be able to participate in one or more training events during the year. The degree of participation will generally be in inverse proportion to the amount of time required and distance involved, as Figure 24 indicates.

**Figure 24
Participation in training approaches**

| Training Approach | Participation Level |
|---|---|
| Single session, on-campus | ← Greater Participation |
| Weekend conference, on-campus | |
| Multiple Sunday nights, on campus | |
| Associational or regional training | ← Moderate Participation |
| Multi-week training course, on-campus | |
| Multiple sessions, off campus | |
| State conference center | Less |
| National conference center | ← Participation |

To make sense of the variety of approaches and content areas, use the needs assessment information to begin to develop an overall training blueprint. Consider the following three-year rotation of courses.

**Figure 25**
**Training Blueprint**

|  | Level 1 Courses<br>Spiritual Formation | Level 2 Courses<br>Bible & Doctrine | Level 3 Courses<br>Sunday School |
|---|---|---|---|
| Year 1 | Spiritual Gifts | Biblical Interpretation | Organization & Admin<br>Outreach & Evangelism |
| Year 2 | Experiencing God | Bible Survey | Principles of Teaching<br>Curriculum Materials |
| Year 3 | Master Life | Baptist Doctrine | Effective Methods<br>Age Level Characteristics |

Each of these courses would be offered over a period of several weeks to several months. Ideally, Level 1 courses should be offered to adult believers who are committed to personal spiritual growth. Level 2 courses should be open to all members, but recommended for potential and new teachers and leaders. Level 3 should be targeted for potential and current teachers and leaders.

**5. Maintain a High Level of Quality** – One of the differences between childhood and adulthood is that children are generally told what to do.

Adults do pretty much what they please or what they perceive to be important. Adults are motivated more by internal than external factors. They will base decisions on what is important to them rather than on what everyone else is doing.

All of this suggests that training sessions had better be interesting and worthwhile if teachers and leaders are to be expected to attend. In my own experience, I have found that most Sunday School workers will attend the first session of a training course simply because I asked them to do so. They will attend the remaining sessions only if they gained benefits from that initial experience.

There are, of course, other reasons why quality is essential. The very nature of our mission demands it. No half-hearted effort on our part will honor Christ or build a strong Sunday School. Quality is essential because our workers need and deserve that quality. We should remember that most of us as pastors and church staff members are paid to work at church. Sunday School teachers and leaders do what they do without financial compensation, as a labor of love. Most work at a job to provide income for their families. When we ask them to take precious time away from those families to receive training, it had better be worthwhile.

**6 Evaluate the Effectiveness** – Evaluation should occur on several levels. It should be both casual and formal. One of the first indicators of the effectiveness of training is attendance at training events. Are workers "burned out" on training? Do they begin a multi-session course only to drop out after the first session or two?

Formal evaluation should be conducted at the conclusion of each training event. Attendees should be given the opportunity to honestly evaluate their experience and suggest ideas for improvement. Visits with experienced leaders after training sessions will be helpful as well. If you are the training leader, convey the idea that you want help in learning how to be more effective.

Learn to measure the long-range benefits of training. Are workers easier to enlist now than before they received training? Are teachers and leaders serving for longer periods of time without discouragement? Are Sunday School classes growing? Are new people being reached?

**Potential Leader Training** – One of the most helpful ways of packaging leadership training is as a course to be offered annually for newly enlisted teachers and leaders prior to the time they begin service. Churches that use this course consistently over a period of several years report little difficulty in finding workers. The idea is simple: Move the enlistment process up approximately six months before the beginning of the new Sunday School year. As part of the enlistment commitment, secure a commitment to be part of potential worker training course.

A number of course models are available, but the suggested format is a 12-week course to be offered in the spring prior to the beginning of the new year in September. The model shown in Figure 26 contains courses and topics from Levels 2 and 3. Participants should have had previous training at Level 1. This model requires two hours per week, with sessions on Sunday morning and Sunday evening. This design is intended to keep the Bible study segments (Level 2) of the course on Sunday morning during the hour normally reserved for Bible study. This portion of the training program is therefore only for those not currently serving. These should be "closed" Sunday School classes, open only to those who had been recommended by the nominating committee. The Sunday evening portion of the course could double as in-service training for those currently. These would be essentially be the Level 3 courses, focusing on aspects of Sunday School work.

## Figure 26
## Potential Leader Training Course

| | 1 | 2 | 3 | 4 | 5 | 6 | 7 | 8 | 9 | 10 | 11 | 12 |
|---|---|---|---|---|---|---|---|---|---|---|---|---|
| **AM** | Unit 1: Introduction to the Bible | | | | | | Unit 4: Baptist Doctrine | | | | Unit 6: Observation & Practice Teaching | |
| **PM** | Unit 2: Principles of Teaching and Learning | | | | | | Unit 3: Understanding Age-Level Characteristics | | | | Unit 5: Utilizing Curriculum Materials | | | |
| | | | | | | | Pre-school | Child-ren | Youth | Adult | Pre-school | Child-ren | Youth | Adult |

**Additional Training Opportunities** – The 3-year Training Blueprint suggested in Figure 25, page 99, should be a general scheduling guide for training courses taught on-campus. This plan will not, however, meet everyone's needs. Consider using several of the approaches suggested below:

**One-day training event.** – This could be a full day mini-training retreat or one or two hours on a Sunday afternoon or evening. The one-session event could help to launch the new Sunday School year, provide an overview of curriculum changes, introduce organizational changes, or cover a variety of other subjects. The advantage is a high degree of participation.

**State or associational training event.** – Many state conventions or associations offer a variety of training events during the year including Sunday School conventions, workshops, and growth clinics. Contact your state Baptist office or local association for a schedule of these events. Because of their brevity, it is usually not difficult to lead a large number of workers to participate.

*Does your church have a training budget? Help with expenses at off-campus events will greatly encourage participation.*

**Associational, state, or national conference centers.** – Many state conventions and associations operate retreat and conference centers where Sunday School training events are scheduled. In addition, LifeWay operates two national conference centers: Glorieta Baptist Conference Center near Santa Fe, New Mexico, and Ridgecrest Baptist Conference Center east of Asheville, North Carolina. At both of these centers, a number of three and four day Sunday School leadership conferences are held throughout the summer months. Although participation by a large number of workers might be difficult, key leaders should be encouraged to participate as often as possible.

# *Teams bonding through planning*

The heart of a successful Sunday School is Wednesday night officers' and teachers' meeting. Look carefully at the table on the next page. It's based on common knowledge. Do you see the problem? Whereas we accept planning as a fact of life in practically any worthwhile endeavor, we generally have the idea that one of the most important responsibilities of all – the making of disciples through regular Bible study – can be done haphazardly. In fact, *it is difficult to imagine a Sunday School being truly effective without regular weekly planning.*

## Figure 27
## Planning Check List

| Which of the following requires planning? | Yes | No |
|---|---|---|
| Development of a weekly network television schedule | ✔ | |
| Lesson plans for a school teachers | ✔ | |
| Offensive strategy for a football team | ✔ | |
| A military assault on a strategic target | ✔ | |
| A workable household budget | ✔ | |
| Design of an interstate highway interchange | ✔ | |
| A growing Sunday School | | ✔ |

**The Benefits of Planning** – Harry Piland, former Sunday School director for Southern Baptists and Minster of Education for a number of large, growing Sunday Schools, suggests the following benefits:[3]

✢ The Weekly Planning Meeting *helps teachers get ready for the Sunday morning teaching sessions*. At least thirty minutes of the time should be devoted to this purpose. In many instances, teachers have become sold on the time-saving value of these sessions. A trained master teacher with Bible study tools can help teachers to understand difficult passages and suggest new ways of applying biblical truths.

✢ The Weekly Planning Meeting provides *an opportunity to deal with problems* related to space, furnishings, upkeep, materials, and supplies, along with other administrative concerns.

✢ The Weekly Planning Meeting *helps workers evaluate their work*, and identify and deal with problem areas.

✢ The Weekly Planning Meeting *helps workers make specific plans for outreach, evangelism, and ministry*. A part of the meeting involves outreach and inreach (ministry) leaders.

✚ The Weekly Planning Meeting *helps build team spirit.* When workers feel they are part of a team, discouragement is minimized.

✚ The Weekly Planning Meeting *helps make Sunday School workers more effective.* Regular meetings provide opportunities for educational staff and others to do mini-training sessions. The mutual accountability that comes as a result of these sessions helps workers to focus more on preparation.

✚ The Weekly Planning Meeting *makes correlation and coordination easier.* The general promotional period provides an opportunity for the pastor, minister of education, or Sunday School director to help all workers see the "big picture."

✚ The Weekly Planning Meeting *helps focus the attention of all workers on evangelism.*

**Making it work** – Consider the following principles in making a Wednesday night officers' and teachers' meeting a success:

**1 Give Sunday School planning prime time.** Successful planning is a matter of setting priorities. It is a well-known trend for churches to build the Wednesday evening programs around a prayer meeting that closely resembles a mid-week worship service, generally minus the invitation. Notice the schedule to the right. Sunday School planning meetings are "sandwiched in" during supper. Many workers are unable to drive home, sometimes change clothes, and drive to church in time to receive maximum benefit from these meetings. Workers generally become discouraged when few show up and when the benefit is marginal.

**Traditional Schedule:**
| | |
|---|---|
| 5:30-6:30 | Fellowship Meal |
| **5:45-6:30** | **Teachers' and Officers' meeting during supper** |
| 6:30-7:30 | Mid-Week Prayer Service |
| 7:30-8:30 | Choir Rehearsal |

Note the second schedule – the one built around a Sunday School planning meeting that receives prime time. Obviously, there would be fewer people in the mid-week prayer service. Here's a question I've started asking pastors: *If you had the choice between [1] maintaining the status quo in terms of Sunday School attendance and prayer meeting attendance over the next five to ten years or [2] losing half your Wednesday night prayer meeting attendance and doubling your Sunday School attendance over the same period of time, which would you choose?*

**Sunday School Priority Schedule:**
| | |
|---|---|
| 5:30-6:30 | Fellowship Meal |
| **6:15-6:30** | **Sunday School Promotion** |
| **6:30-7:30** | **Sunday School Planning Meetings** |
| 6:30-7:30 | Mid-Week Prayer Service |
| 7:30-8:30 | Choir Rehearsal |

> *The alternative to expecting everyone to attend is not expecting them to. Does that really seem better to you, or merely easier?*

**2** **Expect everyone to attend, and work to make it possible.** This, of course, seems idealistic. In a real world, people are busy. Men (and women) have jobs which sometimes take them out of town. Children get sick. Some work with RA's, GA's, children's choirs, or other activities that can compete for the same time slot. There is another alternative to expecting everyone to attend: It is not expecting workers to attend. Do you honestly think that's the better approach?

### Figure 28
### Suggested Schedules for Workers' Meetings

| **Suggested Schedule for Adult and Youth Departments** | |
|---|---|
| 6:15-6:30 | Sunday School General Promotion (all workers) |
| 6:30-6:45 | Department Planning for outreach, prayer, large group time |
| 6:45-7:30 | All teachers using a common curriculum receive lesson overview and helps |
| 6:45-7:30 | Other class and department officers meet with their leaders for outreach, ministry, and fellowship planning. |
| 7:30-8:00 | Make an outreach visit on the way home |

| **Suggested Schedule for Children and Preschool Departments** | |
|---|---|
| 6:15-6:30 | General Sunday School Promotion (all workers) |
| 6:30-6:45 | Divisional Planning for outreach, prayer, special events, and other divisional concerns |
| 6:45-7:30 | Meeting by departments for small and large group planning in rooms |
| 7:30-8:00 | Make and outreach or ministry visit on the way home. One week a month begin this time at 7:00 and schedule more visits. |

| **Suggested Small Church Schedule Using a Common Curriculum** | |
|---|---|
| 6:30-7:30 | Prayer Meeting |
| 6:30-6:45 | Prayer time with all adults |
| 6:45-7:15 | Common Bible study preparation for all workers |
| 7:15-7:30 | Meet by divisions for outreach, ministry, and special event planning |
| 7:30-8:00 | Make a visit on the way home |

| **Suggested Schedule with Less Time Available** | |
|---|---|
| 5:45-6:00 | Meet by departments at supper for general planning |
| 6:00-6:30 | Teachers meet separately |
| 6:00-6:30 | Directors, outreach and officers meet for planning |
| 6:30-7:30 | Prayer Meeting |
| 7:30-8:00 | Make a visit on the way home |

There are several keys to making this expectation close to a reality. The first has already been mentioned: *Give the meeting adequate time as well as a convenient time.* Here are some other suggestions: *[1] Make attendance part of the agreement at the time of enlistment. [2] Relieve Sunday School workers of other leadership duties.* Dennis Parrot, former Minister of Education at Green Acres Baptist Church in Tyler, Texas, established a policy that Sunday School teachers and department officers could not hold any other leadership job in the church. The policy worked.[3] *[3] Make sure the benefit makes the time spent worth-while. [4] Be understanding of the legitimate reasons why workers must miss the meeting at times.* There are times when personal health and family needs must come first. *[5] Let the results speak for themselves.* Your Sunday School will grow. Teachers will be better prepared. More people will receive outreach and ministry contacts.

> *Which of the suggested schedules in Figure 28 would be helpful in your church? How could you improve that schedule?*

**3 Use the time wisely.** Use this time to accomplish every possible benefit. Use the general promotion time for some "mini-training." Make other variations in this time as needed. For example, once a month have a thirty-minute period for training by divisions. Give out an outreach or evangelism assignment to be carried out on the way home.

**Other kinds of planning** – Every Sunday School should be involved in annual planning led by the Sunday School council or general leadership team. The Sunday School council consists of educational staff leadership, Sunday School general officers, division directors, and usually department directors or key teachers from each age division. Annual planning should be conducted to examine growth goals and preparation to meet those goals, to set the direction of the Sunday School for the year, and to develop a calendar of events related to the Sunday School. Monthly Sunday School council planning is the ideal place to make sure those goals and plans are implemented, evaluated, and revised as necessary. It is the best place to monitor the organizational, administrative, and staffing needs of the Sunday School and to create new departments and classes as needed.

## *Blended ministry*

Virtually everything that has been said about training of workers in traditional settings applies to those working in non-traditional settings. Training courses and topics in Levels 1 and 2 would be as useful to a teacher in a missions setting as in a traditional Sunday School class. Several of the level 3 topics, including principles of teaching, knowledge of methods, understanding of age-level characteristics, outreach, and evangelism, would be useful in missions settings as well.

New needs emerge in non-traditional, cross-cultural ministry. Those seeking to serve in these settings often do so outside their own cultural comfort zones. We will address these needs in a fourth level called *cultural orientation*.

> *What other unique training needs might emerge from non-traditional, off-campus Bible study approaches?*

It didn't take me long to realize as I was serving in my first staff church that the unchurched population surrounding my church was very different in terms of attitudes, values, life concerns, lifestyle, and morality from the comfortable middle-class world in which I had grown up and been educated. Baptist churches were not part of their world. We who attended those churches were perceived as being from another world – one they viewed with suspicion and at times dislike. We were the "haves;" they were the "have-nots." The "system" worked for us and against them. From their vantage point, the Baptist church down the street might as well have been a "whites only" country club. They viewed us as people who didn't know them and had no concern for them or their problems. Tragically, there were many times when they were right.

One of the first thing I learned was that the children and teenagers from the unchurched community were a great deal more reachable than were the adults. Children, by nature, are open and trusting. We began to reach them, bring them into the ministries of their church, and care about them in many ways. It dawned on me for the first time that I now had something in common with many adults in the community: We shared a love for their children.

> *What lessons have you learned from working in missions or inner-city settings that would help volunteers in your church?*

During those early years of cross-cultural ministry within my church's geographical community, there would be many other lessons. I had to be shock-proof. When offered a can of beer on a doorstep I had to learn to say no without being offensive. I saw and heard much for which my sheltered life had not prepared me, and I had to learn to look past almost everything to remain focused on the goal. I had to learn to tear down some of those very real barriers that existed by being a real person to them. My price of admission into their world involved spending time with them and demonstrating concern for their children.

It is obvious that training is very necessary for those who feel led to work in someone else's world. This training cannot be charted in the same way that training topics for on-campus ministries can.

**Prison Ministry** – Imagine yourself as a volunteer on your church's prison ministry team. You go out with the pastor and one or two others for a Monday evening worship and Bible study experience. You enter through a series of gates and heavily barred doors. When that final door clangs shut behind you, you find yourself in the same room as the inmates. The same bars that hold them now hold you. The little group from your church is outnumbered 20 to 1 and there are no guards in sight. How do you prepare for such an experience? More importantly, what are the rules? Are there things you are not allowed to do? Can you take mail back and forth as favors to prisoners? *No.* Can you give or loan money or cash checks for them? *Absolutely not.* Are you exempt from searches by prison officials simply because you are ministers? *Not for a minute.*

Training for prison ministry comes essentially in three ways. *First*, the leader of your church's prison ministry should have an orientation session with each new volunteer, telling those individuals what to expect. *Second*, most prison systems require volunteers to take a one- or two-day training course leading to certification. These courses generally address rules to which volunteers must adhere, information about life within that particular prison system, and ways that volunteers can lose their privilege of ministry. *Third,* on-the-job training provides the personal base of experience necessary for effectiveness. In many ways, this is the most valuable training of all. Experience will teach you that the inmates are real people with real problems. They are part of a very unusual culture and at times are part of a prison subculture which is at odds with another subculture within the prison. A combination of observation and experience will teach volunteers how to listen, how to offer counsel, and how to teach in ways they never believed possible.

> **Training for Prison Ministry**
>
> 1. *Initial orientation by leader of church's prison ministry.*
>
> 2. *Mandatory training conducted by prison officials for certification as prison volunteers.*
>
> 3. *On-the-job training*

In many instances, the level of Bible study within a prison class can be conducted at a depth seldom reached in traditional church settings. Many inmates are highly intelligent and highly educated, and some may have had the same *Experiencing God* or *Master Life* course church members have had. Many have experienced a personal transformation that comes through a personal relationship with Christ and are hungry for spiritual knowledge. Nevertheless, they are still there to pay their debt to society. At the end of your Bible study you will leave and they will not.[4]

**Level 4, Cultural Orientation** – It takes only a little while to become comfortable on the mission field. I learned this in Israel many years ago, and more recently in Argentina. Even with continuing language barriers, I still have friends in both of these countries. I want to go back. I have brothers and sisters in both these countries that I probably won't see again until heaven, and I miss them.

Think about the last mission trip you went on. Do you remember the children you taught Bible stories to in the park? Or the elderly people you visited in the low-income housing project? Didn't you in that short time get attached to someone? Weren't you sad to have to leave? *Who are the memories* you left behind?

In ministries such as Outreach Bible Study, *the mission trip continues*. Unlike the type of missions experience that requires travel, *community ministry can be the mission trip that doesn't end.* In community ministry, you leave your mission field for a short time to be in class, at your job, or with your own family, then you return the following week to be with the people you have learned to love. Over a period of time, you begin to see positive changes. You watch children grow. You notice that their behavior changes and their language becomes less offensive. You watch as some come to know Christ. You develop a relationship with parents in hopes that this day will come, and you go into the home to share Christ with the parents by telling them what their child experienced. And it's all right, because you paid the price to gain their trust. You might not win the parents, but you've still got the kids.

If your ministry is with adults, you see their lives begin to change as well. Hope, for many, has now replaced hopelessness, and optimism has replaced cynicisim. Some of your new friends are beginning to get back on their feet. Some have come into a new relationship with Christ, and others have experienced a rekindling of a former relationship that had grown cold. Their desire is now to grow in Christ, to be better parents for their children, and to learn of the purpose for which they were created. You realize how very much you have in common with them.

> *Could your church have a ministry with teenagers who are on the street? High school dropouts? Heavy-metal ravers? If so, how?*

Many otherwise venturesome Christian adults tend to become faint-hearted at the sight of a gang of teenagers on the streets or members of the heavy-metal crowd who attend raves.[5] The sight of orange hair, nose and belly-button rings, and clothing that features offensive pictures or slogans is more than some Christians can take. *Could your church have a ministry with these youth?* Yes. *Would such a ministry be easy?* No. *What sort of Level 4 cultural orientation would be required?* I'm glad you asked.

First, know that it would not be necessary to look, dress, or act like the street-youth you are attempting to reach. In fact, such a tactic would probably be counter-productive. Of greater importance would be your willingness to accept (or at least not be offended by) their appearance. If a teenage girl with purple hair and rings in her lips and eyebrows happens to accept an invitation to visit your youth group, welcome her gladly. Help her to feel comfortable. Like Jesus, look past her outward appearance.

Although over-generalization should be avoided, many in the rock music subculture distrust authority because they perceive that authority has treated them unfairly. Some will tend to associate you with that authority. Learn to establish trust with them by learning their names, shaking their hands, and treating them like real people. They will never hear your message until this trust can be established.

The principle of "taking church to the people" could very well apply to teenagers on the street also. If your church reaches them, it probably will not happen during Sunday School on even on your church campus. You will need to establish a neutral place where they can feel comfortable. This could be something as elaborate as a coffee house or as simple as an empty warehouse. Provide a Christian version of the alternative or rave music they like. You would probably be surprised to learn that you enjoy some of the same activities they enjoy. These might include video games, pool, chess (*yes, chess*), or pinball. Be willing to spend a little time with them. Learn their concerns. Be genuine in your acceptance of them. You might even learn to enjoy their music! You will probably be surprised at their willingness to abide by your rules, including no alcohol, drugs, or tobacco inside the building. Since you're probably not going to get them to break the smoking habit right away, common sense might suggest that you provide a place for them to smoke outside rather than have them leave your premises altogether. Remember that your goal is to share Christ's unconditional love with them. Remember also that this love must be seen in your life long before it can be heard from your lips.

> *Remember that your goal is to share Christ's unconditional love with them. Remember also that this love must be <u>seen</u> long before it can be <u>heard</u>.*

These are the lessons you will learn only by experience, and experiential learning is at the heart of *Level 4* training. You and your partners on your ministry team will learn new and better ways to minister. You'll learn what works and what doesn't. Some of those lessons will be astounding.

> *The most important truth in this* **Blended ministry** *section is probably this: Christ is relevant to every person of every race, every generation, and every culture. Successful ministry, therefore, requires Christians to be as much like Christ as possible.*

## Notes:

## Endnotes

1. Ken Hemphill and Bill Taylor, *Ten Best Practices to Make Your Sunday School Work.* Nashville: LifeWay Press, 2001, p. 111.

2. Adapted from Harry Piland, *Breakthrough: Sunday School Work.* (Nashville: Convention Press, 1990), pp. 161-169.

3. From a workshop led by Dennis Parrott, Director, Sunday School Department for the Baptist General Convention of Texas, in February, 2001.

4. From a conversation with Charles Davenport, Pastor, First Baptist Church of Tulia, Texas, on March 15, 2001.

5. Rave (author's definition): a dance featuring outlandishly loud rock or techno music, a darkened room illumined by strobes and laser lights, and teenagers or young adults who are generally unorthodox in their appearance. While raves have gained the reputation for drug use and underage drinking, some are organized by responsible promoters who employ off-duty police officers to maintain safety and who enforce a no-tolerance policy on drugs and underage drinking.

# Chapter 7
## Providing Facilities and Equipment

I had just begun serving in my first full-time church as a minister of education. The 1500-member church was preparing for a building program, or so I was told. Actually, I wasn't too sure. I studied the attendance record of the church over the past twenty or so years and had learned that there had been no growth for at least that length of time. The worship space was more than ample for our present needs, and the same could be said of the educational facilities, although some re-arranging needed to be done. In time, I found out about the "building program." As it happened, the church had been involved in a building program during its last period of growth in the 1950s. Growth and building buildings became linked in the mind of the pastor and many others in the church. *If we start building again, perhaps we'll start growing again* seemed to be the mind-set. Of course, it didn't work that way.

J.N. Barnette taught us that Sunday Schools cannot outgrow their facilities. *A Sunday School cannot successfully grow beyond the capacity of its building.*[1] Whereas buildings cannot "make" Sunday Schools grow, they can limit or prevent that growth. The building sets the pattern for Sunday School growth. It is unusual for a Sunday School to consistently average more than 80% of its maximum capacity in attendance.

### *Providing adequate space*

The charts on the next page (Figures 29 and 30) show some "Rules of Thumb" for church facilities. These are based on general recommendations for Southern Baptist churches in this country and may not be applicable in every situation. Most of this information was summarized and made available by staff of the Church Architecture Department of the Baptist Sunday School Board, now LifeWay Church Resources.

Let's apply the General Rules of Thumb (Figure 29) to churches. The first has 200 members and needs to provide space for approximately 150 in both Sunday School and worship. A church of this size would need approximately five acres of usable land (not involving utility easements, low-lying areas, steep slopes, or wooded areas). According to the Rules of Thumb, approximately 2,400 square feet are needed for worship space, and another 6,750 square feet are needed for educational space. Both these figures involve the outside dimensions of the buildings and include walls, hallways, stairways, restrooms, and other public areas, in addition to classrooms. Parking space would then be needed for approximately seventy cars, requiring just under an acre.

### Figure 29
### General Rules of Thumb

| Land | 1 acre per 100-125 in attendance + 2-4 acres for recreational purposes |
|---|---|
| Parking | One space for every 2 to 2½ people in attendance at one time; approximately 100 cars may be parked per acre |
| Worship Center | Up to 300 capacity: 15-17 square feet per person<br>Above 300 capacity: 12-18 square feet per person |
| Educational Facilities | First unit building: 30-40 square feet per person (outside dimensions)<br>Small churches: 40-45 square feet per person<br>Large churches with extensive programs: 45-55 square feet per person |

### Figure 30
### Rules of Thumb for Educational Space

**Recommendations in Square Feet per Person in Attendance**

| Age Groups | Room Capacity, based on 70-80% of enrollment ceiling | Classroom Space | Department Assembly Space: | Multi-Use Classrooms / department rooms |
|---|---|---|---|---|
| Preschool, Birth-1 | 7 to 10 | | 35 | |
| Preschool, 2 | 9 to 12 | | 35 | |
| Preschool, 3-5 | 12 to 16 | *15 | 35 | |
| Children, Grades 1-6 | 20 to 24 | *15 | 25 | |
| Youth | 8 to 10 in classroom, 40-50 in department room | 12 | 10 | 18-22 |
| Adult | 15-18 in classroom, 80-100 in department room | 12 | 10 | 18-22 |

\* *This figure is only for smaller Sunday Schools using the class-type organization and department-type Sunday Schools that have small permanent classes within each department.*

The larger of the two churches has some 3,000 members. Worship and Sunday School space would be needed for 1,500 to 1,800 people in attendance. A worship center seating 1,800 would be needed, requiring approximately 30,000 square feet. Adequate Sunday School space would require an additional 90,000 square feet. A minimum of twenty-two acres of land would be required, with thirty or more acres being desirable. Nine acres of parking space would be required.

**Evaluating Space** – Figure 31 shows the process involved in conducting a *space walk*, one of the most effective evaluation tools available.

## Figure 31
## How to Conduct a Space Walk[2]

*Space walk = a physical evaluation of a church's educational facilities to determine functional capacity*

* Begin with the Sunday School enrollment. Chart the enrollment for each unit (class or department). For example,

    |  | Enrollment |
    |---|---|
    | Kindergarten | 16 |
    | 3-4 Grade | 22 |
    | Senior High | 36 |
    | Single Adults | 32 |
    | Senior Adult 1 | 66 |

* Next, find the average attendance for each unit:

    |  | Enrollment | Avg. Attendance |
    |---|---|---|
    | Kindergarten | 16 | 8 |
    | 3-4 Grade | 22 | 12 |
    | Senior High | 36 | 20 |
    | Single Adults | 32 | 12 |
    | Senior Adult 1 | 66 | 30 |

> *Important*: It is necessary to provide space only for the projected maximum attendance, not the enrollment. In addition to the method in Step 3, there are two other ways of determining this figure: [1] Do it physically. Go through the records and look at each unit (class/department) for each Sunday to determine what their highest attendance was for any Sunday during the year. [2] Use the percentage method. Figure 75% of the enrollment as a general rule.

* Determine a figure halfway between enrollment and average attendance for each unit. This is the <u>projected maximum attendance</u>.

    |  | Enrollment | Avg Attendance | Projected Maximum Attendance* |
    |---|---|---|---|
    | Kindergarten | 16 | 8 | 12 |
    | 3-4 Grade | 22 | 12 | 17 |
    | Senior High | 36 | 20 | 28 |
    | Single Adults | 32 | 12 | 22 |
    | Senior Adult 1 | 66 | 30 | 48 |

> *Note:* To determine this figure, add enrollment and average attendance and divide by 2.

*Figure 31, Continued from the previous page*

* Obtain a diagram of the educational building. Identify the location of each classroom and department room.

* Walk through the building and measure <u>each</u> room to determine the square feet, or obtain this information from blueprints.

* Divide the square feet by the square-feet-per-person <u>ratio</u>.[3] This will provide the actual <u>attendance capacity</u>. Compare this figure with the projected maximum attendance figure determined in Step 3.

|  | Enr. | Avg Att | Proj Max Att | Suggested Ratios | Sq. Feet in Rooms | Attendance Capacity |
|---|---|---|---|---|---|---|
| Kindergarten | 16 | 8 | 12 | 35:1 | 300 | 9 |
| 3-4 Grade | 22 | 12 | 17 | 25:1 | 400 | 16 |
| Senior High | 36 | 20 | 28 | 10:1 | 600 | 60 |
| Single Adults | 32 | 12 | 22 | 10:1 | 250 | 25 |
| Senior Adult 1 | 66 | 30 | 48 | 10:1 | 300 | 30 |

* Follow these two steps to determine the enrollment capacity for a particular room: [1] Divide the projected maximum attendance by enrollment. (Ex: For single adults, this figure is .6875, but round it off to .7) [2] <u>Divide</u> the attendance capacity by this decimal (25 / .7 = 36). <u>36</u> is the enrollment capacity for this room.**

> **Note:** In facilities with department rooms that have adjoining classrooms, first figure the total capacity in classrooms (using a ratio of 12:1 for adults) and compare that with the total capacity in the department room. The smaller of the two numbers will indicate the capacity of the department.

* Tabulate the results for all rooms. Figure maximum attendance and enrollment capacity for the Sunday School in its present facility.

* A thorough space walk should indicate the following:
  [1] Areas where present space needs exist.
  [2] Areas where the exchanging of classrooms or department rooms would permit growth.
  [3] The enrollment (or projected maximum attendance) capacity for the building at present.
  [4] The growth possible in the Sunday School without physical changes to the building.
  [5] The maximum enrollment and attendance capacity of the Sunday School with minor remodeling.

---

**Additional guidelines** – When designing or evaluating buildings, consider the following:

★ **Location** – Preschool, senior adult, and special ministries classes and departments should be located on the ground floor unless the building has an elevator. In addition, preschoolers need to be located in a part of the building near young adults. Senior adults need to be fairly close to the worship facility, if possible. Youth, college, and single adults may enjoy their own "space," removed from the preschool and senior adult areas. Children and adults up to age sixty could be located on upper floors.

★ **Shape** – As a general rule, rooms should be approximately two units by three units or three units by four units. For example, a room that is twelve feet in width should have a length of sixteen to eighteen feet. More elongated rooms generally have wasted space; square rooms are usually difficult arrange.

★ **ADA Compliance** – The Americans with Disabilities Act requires in most instances that newly constructed or newly remodeled church facilities meet certain minimum standards. ADA Requirements differ by state and locale but generally include extra wide parking spaces designated as "handicapped," ramps and/or elevators as needed, doors with thirty-six inches of clearance, five feet minimum hallway width, and restrooms equipped with grab bars and specially designed fixtures. These standards do not usually apply to older facilities. Many churches do not address these issues until required to do so.

> *Should churches accommodate the needs of the handicapped only when required to do so by a governmental agency, or should churches provide for persons with special needs because it's the right thing to do?*

## Providing additional space

**Making the most of what you have** – Consider the following low-cost strategies designed to provide additional space until new construction is genuinely needed.

**1 Reassigning rooms.--** From time to time, it is advantageous to shift classes within the building to make better use of existing facilities.
These needs can revealed through a formal space walk or by simple observation  The idea is simple: to eliminate wasted space and permit additional growth. This is possible in churches where classes do not claim ownership of their rooms. I try to discourage the practice of allowing adult classes to remodel or even decorate their own classrooms. This practice can result in a sense of ownership of a classroom that will be counterproductive when the need arises to exchange rooms. When exchanging classrooms, do not move a class a great distance away from other classes in the department, and do not move a class to a part of the building that might be inappropriate for its needs.

## Figure 32
## Dual Sunday School Schedules

| The "Flip-Flop" Schedule ||
|---|---|
| 9:30-10:40 | Early Sunday School, Early Worship |
| 10:50-12:00 | Second Worship, Second Sunday School |

| Dual Sunday School, Single Worship ||
|---|---|
| 8:15-9:25 | Early Sunday School |
| 9:30-10:40 | Worship |
| 10:50-12:00 | Second Sunday School |

| Dual Sunday School and Worship Across Three Time Periods ||
|---|---|
| 8:15-9:25 | Early Sunday School |
| 9:30-10:40 | First Worship, 2nd Sunday School |
| 10:50-12:00 | Second Worship |

**2 Multiple use of facilities.** -- This is usually referred to as a "dual" Sunday School. When carried out properly, the dual Sunday School can virtually double the capacity of the building for all age divisions except preschool. Preschoolers are usually in "extended session" learning experiences during worship services. A dual Sunday School requires two separate Sunday School organizations that provide classes and departments for every group, with only a few exceptions. Possible exceptions could be college or single adults, either of which could benefit from being together during a single time frame. It is essential that both organizations provide for the needs of all ages represented in individual family units. To put this more simply, no family should ever be divided because of a dual Sunday School.

Figure 32 shows three possible schedules, each having its own advantages and disadvantages. In determining the best schedule for your church, consider worship space and parking space as two additional factors that could limit your church's attendance capacity. The first example in Figure 32 assumes that ample parking is available. The second possibility assumes that the worship center is adequate for all those who attend both Sunday Schools. The third plan could have advantages if parking is limited or if some individuals prefer coming early.

The decision to go to a dual Sunday School is one of the most difficult to make. The reason is simple: Many people do not like changes. In going to a dual Sunday School, *everyone* must change. Here are some suggestions for making the dual Sunday School strategy successful:

- Allow ample time for the decision. This is a difficult decision, and not one that can be forced on a congregation. Do your homework; make sure that everyone is aware of the necessity for this plan. Most churches will need as much as a year to make the decision for the dual Sunday School.

- Involve key lay people on a study committee. *Enlist several individuals to serve on the committee whom you know to be against the idea.* This seems counterproductive, but it actually serves three purposes. *First,* their presence forces the committee to do its homework to be able to answer all the objections of the opponents. *Second,* it gives an opportunity to help those who oppose the idea to come to the realization that there is actually no other viable option. *Third,* vocal opponents are generally leaders who have followers. If they become "converted" to the idea, they will bring others along.

- Let everyone be involved in the decision. Make this a church decision, not one made by the staff. Keep the mission of reaching and discipling as many people as possible uppermost in the minds of the congregation.

- Keep family units together. Allow families to choose the Sunday School that is best for them.

- Don't attempt to divide every single adult class. In the oldest adult departments, it is possible to divide the department yet allow classes within the department to remain together. Ladies' Class "A," for example, might choose the early Sunday School and ladies' class "B" might choose the later one.

- Be willing to make adjustments as needed.

- Enlist and train enough workers to maintain the proper department and class sizes and to staff the new organization. Many churches find that 30% to 40% more workers are needed for the dual Sunday School.

**3 Remodel when you can.--** Classrooms that are currently too small can frequently be made usable by removing a partition (wall) separating two classrooms. An experienced carpenter or building engineer should be consulted to point out which walls are non-load bearing and could safely be eliminated. One church consulted an engineer to help devise a plan to eliminate hallways, combine smaller classrooms into larger ones, and make other changes as needed. Even with the addition of new carpeting, the church netted space for an additional one hundred adults in Sunday School for a small fraction of the cost of constructing new space.

*If your church is out of space, have you considered all these possibilities?*

**4 Eliminate tables and other furniture if necessary.--** I did a space walk in a church that was running out of space, or at least that is what

I was told. I found numerous classrooms where eight-foot folding tables were allowed to determine the capacity of the room. An eight-foot table will accommodate no more than eight to ten adults whether it is in a classroom with one hundred square feet or one with twice that amount. *Do not allow furniture to dictate how many people can be put in a room.* This is even true with children, who can use lap boards rather than tables if necessary.

**5 Innovate.**-- Some churches have used worship space, gymnasiums, choir lofts, tents, and even church buses for Sunday School classes.
   This writer even taught a boys' Sunday School class under a shade tree when weather permitted.

**6 Use of portable or temporary buildings.**-- If your church has exhausted the first five suggestions, it's time to consider some long-term solutions. Many churches in the beginning stages of a building program have made good use of temporary portable buildings and adjacent houses for Sunday School space. Some churches are beginning to use "instant buildings" pre-fabricated and moved on-site for use as worship, recreational, and multi-use facilities. Southcliff Baptist Church in Fort Worth, Texas, purchased a 70 by 120 foot building for use as a temporary worship center. When this 700-seat worship facility is no longer needed, it will be sold and moved to another location. The Canadian-based company that developed this technology can erect a building in a parking lot or vacant lot in as little as six weeks. The cost of the buildings is approximately $20 per square foot, a fraction of the cost of permanent structures. These buildings are durable and able to withstand 150 mile-per-hour winds and snow.[4]

**7 Cell groups.**-- In most instances, home-based Bible study groups belong more in the ***Blended ministry*** sections of this book than in the traditional sections. Many new churches, however, are using home-based cell groups as start-up strategies. Some churches keep the cell groups, preferring this approach to traditional educational buildings. A few churches are using cell groups as interim growth strategies. These Bible study units are usually considered part of the main Sunday School. They meet in diverse locations, but their members generally participate in a corporate worship experience. The rapid rise of cell groups is due partly to the realization that buildings have been over-emphasized.

**New Construction** – There are times when none of the approaches above are workable and new construction is the best plan. Among the indicators are substantial and persistent growth, a healthy financial base, and members who are highly committed to the ministry goals of the church. Churches should never build to attempt to cause growth, only to contain and permit it. Growth momentum is necessary when going into a building program and during the process of construction. Several of the strategies listed above could prove helpful in permitting this momentum. In developing a plan for a building consider the following:

- **Need** -- Could any of the interim strategies (above) be considered permanent solutions to growth needs?

- **Purpose** – What needs should an educational building serve? Should recreational space be included? Should the building be multi-use? Which age groups need to be served through this project?

- **Type of construction** – Zoning requirements could help to determine the type of construction needed. Some churches in rural areas and other areas where zoning restrictions are not a problem use a free-span steel method with a standard drywall interior. Construction costs are kept to a minimum. Interior work can sometimes be done by volunteers. In other instances, a turn-key project is advisable, one that would be seen as an asset to the community. Depending on the location, costs can range from $75 to $100 per square foot.

- **Design** – A number of church-oriented design firms are available through the country. The Church Architecture Department at LifeWay Christian Resources has a team of four architects who assist churches in a variety of ways. For new congregations planning their first permanent home, the department provides site studies and preliminary building drawings. For established congregations, assistance is geared toward space evaluation, master site planning, and construction documents (blueprints) for new buildings. In the master site planning process, property needs, budget realities, and ministry goals are evaluated. The cost of these services is on a sliding scale based primarily on current or projected size of the congregation. The department produces the book *Planning and Building Church Facilities* by Gwen McCormick (Convention Press). In addition, the Church Architecture Department offers help with financing of construction through their *Together We Build* program.

- **Construction Costs** – Recall from Figure 29 that educational buildings normally require 45 to 55 square feet per person, based on outside dimensions. Simpler buildings for smaller congregations often require 30 to 40 square feet per person. An educational facility to accommodate an attendance of 500 would normally require approximately 25,000 square feet at an approximate cost of $75 per square foot for the actual building, or $1,875,000. This is not the total cost, however. Architectural fees, furnishings, landscaping, and other contingencies can require 25 to 30% of the total cost. The $75 per square foot cost is actually close to $100, and the cost of the building has risen to $2,500,000.

> **Consider this:**
> 30% of the cost of a project to be raised in cash, prior to construction, with another 30% to be raised in pledges to be paid off within a three-year period. The balance of 40% could then be financed over a period of no more than 15 years.

- **Financing Considerations** – It is at times more difficult for a church than for an individual to obtain financing for a major building project. Banks and other lending institutions are hesitant to foreclose on a church. The church loan department of the Baptist Foundation of Oklahoma recommends that churches borrow no more than two to two and a half times the annual budget of the church. Debt retirement should be no more than 25 to 30 percent of a church's budget. It is imperative that as much be raised in cash or pledges as possible.

## Age-Level space and equipment needs

In the following sections, we'll apply some of the information related to space requirements from Figure 30, and look at some possible room configurations.

**Figure 33**
**Adult Sunday School Department, Large Church**

| Classroom 252 SF | Classroom 216 SF | Classroom 216 SF |
| Classroom 216 SF | Department Assembly Room 936 SF | |
| Classroom 216 SF | | |

◆ **For Adults.--** For classes, twelve square feet per person is recommended. In department rooms, the recommendation is ten square feet per person. In adult rooms where flexible configurations are used (combinations of large and small groups in Bible study), eighteen to twenty-two square feet per person is recommended. All of these ratios are for people in attendance. Space is needed, therefore, for the *projected maximum attendance* (see Figure 31). If adult classes have an enrollment ceiling of twenty-five, this would generally translate to a projected maximum attendance of around eighteen. Based on twelve square feet per person, the optimum size for an adult classroom would be 216 square feet, or a room 12' x 18'. The largest department room should accommodate approximately ninety (75% of 125, the suggested enrollment ceiling). This translates to 900 square feet based on ten square feet per person, or a room measuring approximately 24' x 36'.

Figure 33 is a floor plan for an adult department with the maximum recommended enrollment. The capacity of the classrooms roughly equals the capacity of the assembly room. One classroom is a bit larger than the others.

◆ **For Youth, Grades 7-12.--** The same general floor plan as indicated in Figure 33 could be used for youth if it were scaled back just a bit.

The suggested enrollment for youth is sixty in departments and twelve in classes. (Refer to Figure 7, page 59). The projected maximum attendance in the youth department would be approximately forty to fifty, with approximately 450 square feet, or a room approximately 18' x 27'. Classrooms would require space for nine (108 square feet), or a room no smaller than 9' x 12'.

◆ **For Children, Grades 1-6.--** Children's departments have a suggested enrollment maximum of thirty, including workers. Space should be provided, therefore, for approximately twenty-four. Using the figure of twenty-five square feet per person, 600 square feet of space would be required, or a room measuring approximately 20' x 30'. (See Figure 34). The open room concept depicted in this floor plan allows for maximum flexibility and is preferred by many children's educators.

For older children's departments that have permanent small groups (classes), approximately fifteen to eighteen square feet per person is needed in the classrooms as well as the

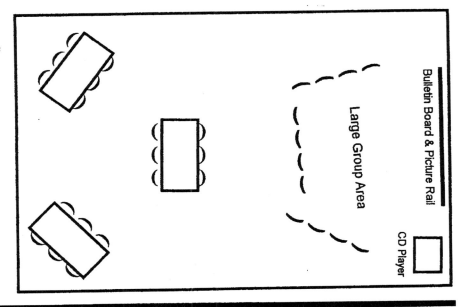

**Figure 34
Children's Department Utilizing Open-Room Teaching**

assembly room. Children, though smaller, are more active and thus require more space.

It is not necessarily true that children learn best when sitting in a chair at a table *all the time,* so alternatives should be provided to standard furnishings. Chair heights should be 12" to13" for first and second graders, 14"-15" for third and fourth graders, and 15"-16" for fifth and sixth. Pianos are seldom needed, but CD players would be helpful. Tables should be adjustable in height and set to 10" above the chair height. Children's rooms should be clean and attractive, with adequate lighting and good ventilation. Wall surfaces should be light in color and free from clutter. Visible teaching materials should be only from the current unit of study. Only necessary pieces of equipment should be left in the room. Carpeting is preferred to tile since children will occasionally be on the floor.[5]

◆ **For Preschoolers, Birth-Pre-first grade** – The needs of preschoolers differ widely by age. In the limited space available on these pages, it is not possible to go into adequate detail about rooms or furnishings. Resources are available through the Preschool Sunday School consultants at LifeWay Christian Resources and through the preschool and children's consultants on the staffs of many state conventions. Numerous ideas for room arrangement and design exist in published form. Figure 35 on the next page shows two of many possible groupings. The diagrams show views of two preschool rooms in smaller churches that combine several ages together. For more information, consult *Preschool Sunday School for a New Century* by Cindy Lumpkin and Thomas Sanders as well as other current resources available through that department and LifeWay Christian stores.

## *Blended ministry*

Of all the topics dealt with in this book thus far, the ***Blended ministry*** section dealing with facilities has less in common with the traditional on-campus church than any other. Square foot ratios are often unimportant in community missions settings, as are chair height, room size, or the placement of the CD player. Floor plans such as those depicted in the section above simply don't exist.

In prison ministry, for example, one Bible class may have one hundred or more men in one room. Prison ministry leaders cannot worry about enrollment ceilings or square foot ratios. The common room set aside for educational purposes and at times designated as a chapel will have to do.

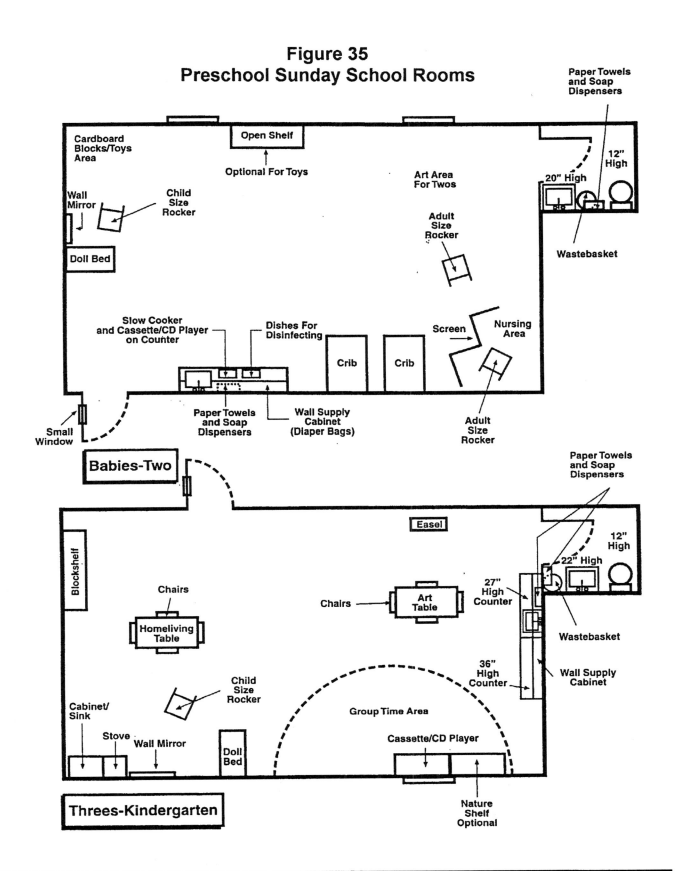

Mission Arlington is an excellent example of two very important principles at work. Bible study classes meet in every conceivable place, including apartment houses, recreation rooms, mobile home parks, schools, and nursing homes. When asked how they came up with the locations, the associate director of the center replied, *We really don't have to. God provides them for us.* This is partly because their reputation has grown to the extent that they are known all over their city. Apartment house managers frequently call Mission Arlington staff to request a Bible study or an after-school program for children. It is important to learn what the ground rules are when beginning in a new location. At times it might be necessary for an apartment resident to invite a Bible study group to come in. At other times, facilities such as club rooms are provided by apartment management. Learn to work with the management and follow their rules. Gain their trust by letting them see the results of your ministry over a period of time.

> *Two important principles:*
> ➤ Adapt what you have
> ➤ God will provide what you need

Don Lane of Amarillo's City Church reported that there have been times that God has provided an entire church facility for them to use. Several older neighborhood churches were at the point of closing their doors. These were traditional churches that failed to adapt their style of ministry to the needs of the community. On two or three occasions, the church properties were deeded over to City Church. Leaders of both City Church and Mission Arlington report corporate donations of large buildings or tracts of land as tax write-offs.

The Hispanic mission of Shawnee's Immanuel Baptist church is an example of the use of non-traditional facilities. The church planting strategy team has opted for starting cell groups in homes rather than using traditional church facilities. Reasons for this have already been discussed. Benefits of this approach include relatively unlimited potential for growth and a biblical understanding of the church as a fellowship rather than a place. In addition, the cell groups will help Hispanics without proper documentation to maintain a low profile until they become comfortable with their new Christian fellowship and learn to trust its leadership.

The possibilities for facilities are endless. Allow God to lead. Learn to toss aside the traditional methods and improvise. Learn to work with what you have. God will give to every group of believers adequate resources to use in being obedient to Him.

# Notes

# Endnotes

1. Generally, this law still holds true. Recent trends toward multiple use of buildings such as dual Sunday School and non-traditional places for Bible study classes have tended to modify this law in some instances.

2. *How to Conduct a Space Walk.* ©2000, Robert A. Dawson, Shawnee, Oklahoma.

3. See Taylor and Hanks, *Sunday School for a New Century,* LifeWay Press 1999, p. 167.

4. For additional information, go to the website of Sprung Instant Buildings, www.sprung.org, or the website of Southcliff Baptist Church, www.southcliff.org.

5. These suggestions are adapted from Paula Stringer, Crayons, Computers, & Kids. (Nashville: Convention Press, 1996), pp. 46-49.

# Part 3:
# Changing Lives

**Introduction**

**Chapter 8: Using Curriculum, Changing Lives**
- Developing a curriculum plan
- Teaching for transformation
- Blended ministry

**Chapter 9: Getting to Work: Outreach, Evangelism, and Ministry**
- The Sunday School and outreach
- The Sunday School and evangelism
- The Sunday School and ministry
- The Jesus model: Putting it all together
- Blended ministry: Are we talking about the social gospel?

# Introduction to Part 3

Without these last two chapters, it is doubtful that we would be any better off than we are right now. We have a sense of our history, and that history has taught us much. We can look within our congregations then out into our communities and conclude that something is wrong. We're not reaching the people we're supposed to be reaching. These were the lessons of *Part 1: Examining Past and Present.*

We even know most of the techniques and principles that could be applied to make things better. We know, for example, that we need prospect files, well-staffed organizations, and well-trained workers. We understand the need for classrooms of the appropriate size and of furnishings to go in those rooms. It's possible, in fact, that we might have even given too much priority to facilities. All these principles and methods were with us throughout most of the twentieth century. These methods and principles made up most of *Part 2: Blending Ministries*. If you're like me, however, there's something in Part 2 that bothered you. Perhaps you were reminded of the many that we're not reaching, and that furthermore we're not even really trying.

That brings us to *Part 3: Changing Lives*. In these last two chapters, we'll begin to examine some tools and principles related to getting to work and doing those things we know to do. Chapter 8 focuses on curriculum. More than the printed materials ordered every three months from a Christian publishing house, *curriculum* really refers to what happens in a teaching-learning situation. What does happen when we study God's word? Do we allow the truths of the Bible to transform and re-order our lives? Is it possible that we could see this same transformation within the lives of the homeless, the drug addicts, the alcoholics, and the "street kids" all around us? The answer might surprise you.

In Chapter 9, we'll put back together some things we've deliberately kept separated in our churches and our ministries: outreach, evangelism, and ministry. We'll learn from the ministry of Jesus that these concepts cannot be separated. The application of evangelism combined with ministry will make possible the **Blended ministries** we've seen throughout this book.

As you study these last two chapters, allow one question to be asked in your mind and answered through your response to this study: *Isn't it time?*

– *Bob Dawson*

# Chapter 8
## Using Curriculum, Changing Lives

*Do not be conformed to this age, but be transformed by the renewing of your mind, so that you may discern what is the good, pleasing, and perfect will of God. (Romans 12:2, HCSB)*

Most of the principles in this book have dealt with the growth and health of the Sunday School organization. An emphasis has been on maintaining a healthy organization, staffed with trained leadership that can function as a team. It is possible that if we stop there and go no further we could have a large well-staffed organization, but one made up of members who are living powerless lives. To have a large, well-led Sunday School organization was never Christ's purpose. When He ascended into heaven, in a very real way He left His body on this earth. We are that body. We are to continue the work which Christ started until He returns to bring it to completion. Christ, either directly or through the apostles, gave us insight into what must happen in order for us to carry out this work: We must *abide in Him,* for unless we do so, we can *do nothing* (from John 14:5). We will be witnesses of Christ to a lost world, having been empowered by His Holy Spirit (from Acts 1:8). As believers, it is our destiny to be conformed to the likeness and image of Christ (from Romans 8:29). We are to seek and possess the same mind-set and attitude as Christ (from Philippians 2:5). A good organization can help, but organization in itself can accomplish very little. We must be taught the spiritual truths necessary for us to be Christlike in our daily lives. We must go beyond the *elementary teachings* about Christ and become *mature* in Him (from Hebrews 6:1).

> *Do our members think more about "going to church" or about becoming Christ-like? Are we caught up more in the activities of the institution, or in the mission of Christ?*

This process of growing up a family of believers into true spiritual maturity who are living out the Christ-life in their world can be helped along by the careful selection of curriculum resources and the understanding of ways to teach for spiritual transformation. It is the purpose of this chapter to help the reader go beyond the focus upon the organization to a focus on teaching our people to be like Christ.

## *Developing a curriculum plan*

The selection of curriculum resources is one of the most important decisions Sunday School leadership can make. Much is involved. Curriculum selection grows out of the needs of people to advance in their spiritual lives. Some are not yet believers; these need a basic Bible study plan capable of providing the necessary foundation. Some are Christians who need to begin growing and ordering their lives around Christ. Some have matured to the point that they are ready to learn to be teachers and leaders of others in the congregation. A comprehensive curriculum plan must reflect all of these needs. The plan must include everyone, regardless of their age, culture, race (language), or maturity level. It must provide foundational truths for young children, it must be challenging for youth and adults, and it must be relevant to everyone.

The development of a curriculum plan includes much more than deciding which curriculum series or which publisher to use, because one size does *not* fit all. Once the needs of learners have been assessed, a basic curriculum line should be selected. In making this selection, many factors must be considered.

> *Don't place your trust in a curriculum series to provide what you need; rather, trust God to show you the resources to use.*

**Who decides?** And how is that decision made? Some churches select a curriculum series or publisher by vote of the congregation. Other churches make this decision based on denominational loyalty. Both of these approaches are flawed. Neither the church body nor the editorial staff of a publishing house can possibly know the ever-changing needs of your people. No one can *really* provide assurance that the materials being used now will be doctrinally sound or educationally appropriate ten years from now. It is very little better to ask the pastor or minister of education to select curriculum materials on their own. Every church needs a curriculum selection, review, and evaluation process that includes feedback from teachers. The Sunday School general leadership team is probably the best group to conduct this process.

**Types of Curriculum.** Many different types of curriculum resources are available. It is very probable that most churches will select from two or more of the following:

- **Dated, content-oriented.--** An example of this curriculum is *Explore the Bible*, published by LifeWay Church Resources.[1] Curriculum of this nature frequently presents books of the Bible or major portions of Scripture over a period of time ranging from several weeks to several months. Its focus is on the meaning of the biblical passage, with a secondary focus on application. It is intended for mature Christians desiring a "deeper" Bible study experience.

- ☐ **Dated, application-oriented.**-- The *Family Bible Study* series produced by LifeWay Church Resources is an application-oriented curriculum line. The series is available for all ages from nursery through senior adults and provides common Scripture texts, thus enabling families to engage in lesson study together. Curriculum materials of this type are generally theme-oriented or topical, and they emphasize life application more than content exploration. Family Bible Study is well suited for younger learners, new believers, families, and anyone preferring an emphasis on applicaiton.

- ☐ **Undated, topical.**-- Examples here include biblical studies on Christian living, selected biblical books, parenting, men's and women's issues, Christian doctrine, and Bible survey. Publishers such as NavPress specialize in this type of study.

- ☐ **New believers.**-- A type of topical study, the focus here is upon the basic needs of new Christians or new church members. The *Survival Kit* series, *Now That I'm a Christian*, and *Basics for Baptists*, all offered by LifeWay, are examples.

- ☐ **Emerging leaders.**-- A number of churches are using these materials as a specialized Sunday School experience for potential teachers and leaders. Examples might include doctrinal overviews or spiritual gifts studies.

- ☐ **Self-written curriculum.**-- The "do-it-yourself" approach is one that is growing in popularity as a

---

### Self-Written Curriculum
#### Advantages
+ Avoidance of doctrinal difficulties (unless you create some others in the process)
+ Ability to meet the needs of many (but not all) of your learners. Remember that their needs differ widely.
+ Ability to address specific issues
+ Cost savings (if you don't count your time and salary)

#### Disadvantages
- Lack of adequate depth in a wide area of biblical knowledge. (Many curriculum writers and editors have a Ph.D. in a biblical field)
- Lack of expertise in educational methodology and curriculum design (Many writers of teaching procedures are trained as educators and have graduate degrees in their field.)
- A major commitment of time that could be invested in other ways

means of meeting the unique needs of learners in a local church. This possibility should be considered as a last rather than a first choice. Many have found it beneficial to write a single lesson on a particular subject or event in the life of a church rather than an entire series.

**Characteristics of Good Curriculum.** Howard P. Colson and Raymond M. Rigdon list seven characteristics of good curriculum:[2]

1. *Biblical and theological soundness.* Does the curriculum material present genuine Christianity? What is the theological reference, touchstone, or point of view of the curriculum designers, editors, and writers?

2. *Relevance.* Are the themes, passages, and instructional objectives suited to the nature and needs of learners in their current situation?

3. *Comprehensiveness.* Does the curriculum include all that is essential in the scope and all that is essential to the spiritual growth and development of the learner?

4. *Balance.* Does the curriculum avoid both underemphasis and overemphasis of the various parts that make it up?

5. *Sequence.* Is the presentation of the parts (units, themes, books) of the curriculum in the best order for learning?

6. *Flexibility.* Is the curriculum easily adaptable to the individual differences of the learners, adaptable to churches of different types, and adaptable to the varying abilities and needs of both teachers and learners?

7. *Correlation.* Are the various parts of the church's overall curriculum plan properly related to each other? For example, is Sunday School curriculum complementary to and supportive of the curriculum of missions education?

Curriculum *scope* should be added to this list. "The scope of curriculum is that which is appropriate to be dealt with in the curriculum. It is more than subject matter. ...It really means subject matter in relation to experience."[3] Scope is very much like a diet that is based on the individual's nutritional needs. In curriculum design, scope should consider the age, experience, and life situation of the focal group of learners.

**Selecting a Publisher / Curriculum Line.** If the matter of curriculum selection is not simply a matter of "denominational loyalty," then consider the following:

- **Doctrinal content.--** Some curriculum lines use a doctrinal frame of reference as a touchstone for writers and editors. For example, Sunday School curriculum materials published by LifeWay Christian Resources must adhere to the *2000 Baptist Faith and Message.* Other publishers use statements such as the New Hampshire Confession of Faith. Still others simply employ writers from within an evangelical tradition but make no further requirements. Regardless, the responsibility for doctrine should never release the church's selection committee from the responsibility of making certain that the material is doctrinally sound.

- **Editorial policy and control.--** It is wise to determine who within the publishing house sets policy and administers doctrinal and educational content of the curriculum materials being purchased. To whom are these individuals accountable? Does this process allow for and acknowledge feedback from those who use the curriculum?

- **Educational approach.--** Does the educational methodology of the materials being considered acknowledge the needs and capabilities of the learners? For preschoolers and young children, is the material more foundational or cognitive in its orientation? Does it teach facts or build pre-concepts? For older children, youth, and adults, does the material balance content and application? Are follow-through activities suggested? Are a variety of learning styles such as verbal, visual, and kinesthetic employed?

- **Age-level scope.--** Is the age-level scope appropriate to the learners who will be using the materials? Some curriculum lines are "youth" only. Others include all ages with the exception of children under the age of 3. How closely "graded" is the material? Many curriculum lines do not distinguish between young and senior adults, married and single adults, first graders and sixth graders, and so forth.

- **Availability of resources.--** What is available for use by those who will teach the materials? Is there anything beyond a "teachers' book?" Are dated commentaries available? Are there resource kits containing visually-oriented or interactive materials? Are web updates available to keep materials current? Are there teaching pictures for preschoolers and children? Is the material dependent on the use of CD-players, computers, or even overhead projectors? Are learners given adequate resources with which to prepare?

- **Training and support.--** Does the publisher work with a team of consultants on the state or local level who can train teachers and leaders in the use of the materials? Curriculum lines published by LifeWay are supported by conference leaders and consultants on the national, state, and at times the associational level. Are instructional or informational web sites provided?

- **Cost.--** Finally, is the material affordable by the local church? Some churches keep the cost down with "bare bones" orders including books for learners and teachers, and nothing more. Some materials, however, are marketed as "kits" which do not allow for or encourage this approach. A comparative study of curriculum materials and their costs from several publishers could prove helpful.

## Figure 36
## Curriculum Information Chart[4]

| Publisher | Age Scope / Denominational Affiliation | Contact Information | Doctrinal Statement Available? |
|---|---|---|---|
| Child Evangelism Fellowship | Older preschool and elementary / Interdenominational, evangelical | Child Evangelism Fellowship<br>PO Box 348<br>Warrenton, MO 63383-0348<br>1-636-456-4321<br>1-888-748-7710<br>http://www.cefinc.org | Yes, online |
| Children's Ministry International | Older preschool and elementary / Interdenominational, evangelical | CMI<br>2368 Main Street<br>Suite 3<br>Tucker, GA<br>1-888-345-4264<br>http://www.childministry.com | Yes, online |

*Continued from the previous page*

| Publisher | Age Scope / Denominational Affiliation | Contact Information | Doctrinal Statement Available? |
|---|---|---|---|
| David C. Cook | All / Interdenominational, evangelical | David C. Cook Church Ministries<br>4050 Lee Vance View<br>Colorado Springs, CO 80918<br>1-719-536-0100<br>http://www.cookministries.com | Yes, online |
| Gospel Light Publications | All / Interdenominational, evangelical | Gospel Light Publications<br>2300 Knoll Dr.<br>Ventura, CA 93003<br>1-800-4GOSPEL<br>http://www.gospellight.com | Yes, online |
| LifeWay Church Resources | All / Multiple curriculum series / Southern Baptist | LifeWay Church Resources<br>127 Ninth Avenue, North<br>Nashville, TN 37234<br>1-800-458-2772<br>http://www.lifeway.com | Yes, link to 2000 Baptist Faith and Message |
| NavPress (Navigators) | Adult, topical / Interdenominational, evangelical | NavPress<br>P.O. Box 35002<br>Colorado Springs, CO 80935<br>1-800-366-7788<br>http://www.navpress.com | None online |
| Scripture Press - See David C. Cook | | | |
| Summit Ministries | Youth / Interdenominational, evangelical | Summit Ministries<br>P. O. Box 207<br>Manitou Springs, CO 80829<br>1-719-685-9103<br>http://www.summit.org | None online |

## *Teaching for transformation*

*But be doers of the word and not hearers only, deceiving yourselves.* (James 2:22, HCSB)

The failure of many if not most Christians to be Christ-like in their daily lives is considered by many to be the greatest hindrance to local, national, and international evangelization. Is it possible to attend a weekly Bible study class and *not* be transformed? Is it possible to hear repeatedly Christ's exhortation to Christian unity, John's exhortation to Christian love, and Paul's exhortation to Christ-likeness and *not* be radically changed? Is it possible that after nearly 2000 years many of Christ's "followers" more closely resemble the Scribes and Pharisees than Christ (see Figure 2, p. 19), whom they've gone on record as asking to be their Lord? Unfortunately, tragically, yes. Obviously so. I have knocked on many doors and talked with many lost people only to be told, *What's so special about being a Christian? The ones I know are no better than I am.* Or *Your church doesn't need any more hypocrites. It has enough already.* It is difficult to get past this and turn the conversation to Christ. It has been said that *Christians are people who read the Bible. Lost people read Christians.* It is the job of Christian teachers to help their learners to be more like Christ. First, they exemplify Christ-likeness. Second, they focus on the mission.

> *Christians read the Bible. Lost people read Christians.*

### The Mission of Christian Teaching

The process of helping another person toward Christ-likeness does not come automatically. Teachers must first of all have an intimate, experiential knowledge of Christ and a growing knowledge of Scripture. They must know their learners: their development, their learning characteristics, their needs, and the obstacles they face. Teachers must have specialized training regardless of the ages of their learners.

**Preschoolers: First steps.** What can a preschooler learn? More than most adults think. Even before they learn to talk, preschoolers can learn about God's love through those around him. Words such as *God*, *Jesus*, and *Bible*, when used frequently by loving teachers and associated with pleasant experiences, are bound forever in the preschooler's mind.[5] Learning activities for preschoolers are centered in nine content areas, as shown in Figure 37.[6]

**Figure 37
Preschool Content Areas**

1. God
2. Jesus
3. Bible
4. God's Creation
5. Church
6. Self
7. Family
8. Community
9. World

Specifically, preschoolers during their first two years can learn that God loves them, that God made them, that Jesus was born, that Jesus helped people, that the Bible is a special book about God and Jesus, that the Bible has stories about Jesus, that the Bible helps us to know the right things to do, that God made plants and animals, that God made food, that people at church help each other, that people at church love God and Jesus, that they are special, that they are important, that they can make choices, that they can talk to God, that they are members of a family, that God gave them parents, and that they can learn to help others.

Children from age three through pre-kindergarten can add to the knowledge of their earlier years. They can learn that God hears them when they pray, that God gives rules because He loves them, that Jesus is God's Son, that God sent Jesus to earth, that Jesus' teachings apply to them, that the stories in the Bible are true and the people are real, that God made the earth and its weather, that people at church have different tasks, that people give their money at church, that going to church is important, that people are more important than anything else that God created, that God has planned for them to grow in a certain way, that they can praise God, that they can obey their parents and their rules, that other people are important to God, that missionaries tell people about God, and that God loves people around the world.

Kindergarten children can learn that God is real, that He is the ruler of the world, that He has a plan for their life, that they should obey the teachings of Jesus and follow His example, that Jesus died on the cross, that He was raised from the dead and lives in heaven, that the Bible tells what God is like, that the Bible tells that Jesus is alive, that churches are people and not buildings, that God gave them abilities to think and work, that they are happiest when they obey God's teachings, that they can make their home happier because they are obedient, that some people are different in their language and culture, that they can respect people even though they might be different, and that they can learn about people in other countries.[7]

Preschoolers need teachers who experience God's love in their daily lives, who understand their developmental needs and learning capabilities, and who exemplify the concepts they are teaching. Their teachers must help them to learn through their senses, through their curiosity, through "hands-on" experiences, through relationships, through imitation, through play, through repetition, and through words.[8]

**Children: Growing up to be like Jesus.** Children come to us from a variety of backgrounds. Many have the privilege of growing up in a Christian family with both parents present. Some come from broken families, either Christian or non-Christian. Some grow up in unchurched families in which they have no opportunity to learn about Jesus. Anthony was like that. As a nine-year old from a middle-class family, Anthony had no real knowledge of Jesus. The only times he ever heard Jesus' name mentioned were in curses or occasionally when his grandmother took him to the Catholic church. I had the opportunity of changing that. I sat down with Anthony during a Royal Ambassador meeting just after he started attending. I told him the basic facts: that Jesus was God's Son who came to earth, that Jesus lived a sinless life, and that He died on the cross to take the punishment for sins that we deserved. I told him that Jesus was buried but that He arose from the dead on the first Easter Sunday morning, and that He is alive today. Anthony's initial reaction? He thought Jesus was "cool." Several months later, Anthony invited Jesus into his heart.

Despite their diverse backgrounds, children have a common need: to know Jesus more fully, in anticipation of the time when, like Anthony, they can invite Him to be their Savior and Lord. The teacher of children must constantly be aware of that fact and make it part of every lesson preparation.

Learning for children can be divided into three broad categories: cognitive, affective, and psychomotor.[9] The *cognitive* dimension focuses on growing in knowledge and understanding. Children need basic Bible facts, but as they grow older they need to understand the principles being taught. They need to be challenged to think, explore, imagine, and dig deeper. They have a lot of "why" and "how" questions that need answers. A part of understanding is application: not just what the Bible means but what it *means to them*.

*Affective* learning relates closely to application because it has to do with changed attitudes, feelings, and even emotions. Children can learn to care. They can learn to be understanding of and care about those who are different physically, culturally, or racially. They can learn about how people in Bible times might have felt, and gain insight into their own feelings.

A change in attitude can prompt children to action. This is what the *psychomotor* dimension of learning is about. Psychomotor learning has a classroom dimension through the involvement of children in activity-oriented learning experiences. Researchers have discovered that children may remember a small percentage of what they hear, a greater percentage of what they both see and hear, but most of what they hear as they are engaged in a related activity, such as making a map, creating art, planting seeds, dramatizing a Bible story, or using puppets. Psychomotor learning has a dimension outside the classroom as well. One teacher regularly asks her fifth graders what they plan to do as a result of that day's lesson.

Children need the opportunity to develop Bible skills. The Bible Skills Chart (Figure 38) outlines skills which should be mastered at each age level. Scripture memorization is not referenced on this chart. Please consider the following:

**Should children memorize Scripture?** Yes. Definitely. Some Christian educators might disagree, particularly with younger children who are still struggling with learning to read. Children of all ages should learn the practical advantages of "hiding God's word in their hearts." The following guidelines should help.

- ♦ **Keep the verses simple**, especially for younger children. Make sure they understand the meaning of what they are learning.
- ♦ **Exemplify the practice of memorizing Scripture** by quoting verses (especially the "memory verse") by memory. Don't do this to impress anyone, but to show the importance of memorization. Children need to know you're not asking them to do something you're unwilling to do.
- ♦ **Give examples of the benefits** of Scripture memory by sharing experiences in which God reminded you of a verse to deal with (or avoid) a difficult situation.
- ♦ **Prioritize practice** by allowing time for Scripture memorization every week.
- ♦ **Encourage participation** in activities such as Bible Drill and other programs which emphasize an age-appropriate memorization plan.[10]
- ♦ **Reward children's efforts** in meaningful ways.

## Figure 38
## Bible Skills Chart[11]

| Level One: Grades 1-2 | Level Two: Grades 3-4<br>All Level 1, plus... | Level Three: Grades 5-6<br>All Levels 1 and 2, plus... |
|---|---|---|
| ★ Know that certain stories and verses are in the Bible<br>★ Recognize that the Bible is a book from God<br>★ Name the two main divisions of the Bible<br>★ Locate certain books in the Bible and be familiar with what they contain<br>★ Locate the contents pages in the Bible and be able to locate books<br>★ Say aloud the names of Bible books in which the lesson is found<br>★ Name and find the four Gospels<br>★ Understand how to read a Bible reference | ★ Pronounce the names of Bible books<br>★ Locate most Bible books<br>★ Use the contents page to locate any book<br>★ Read a Bible reference<br>★ Find a chapter and verses called for in a reference<br>★ Recognize and know the basic groupings (divisions) of the Old and New Testament books<br>★ Identify books with some of the men God used to write the Bible<br>★ Identify key books by the information contained in them. For example, Genesis tells about creation; Exodus gives the 10 Commandments; Matthew, Mark, Luke, and John tell about Jesus' life. | ★ Locate all the books in the Bible<br>★ Know all the books in order<br>★ Locate a Bible reference and find information from it<br>★ Identify and locate key Bible books according to the information contained in them. For example, the story of the early church is in Acts.<br>★ Find the names of major Bible people in books where their stories are recorded<br>★ Be able to locate from memory often-used Bible passages and memory verses<br>★ Recognize the basic groupings of the Old and New Testaments<br>★ Recognize the basic divisions of the Old and New Testament books; identify all books in the divisions |

Children need to be able to relate personally to their teachers. Teachers need to be willing to get to know their children outside the classroom. Children need to feel comfortable asking their teachers difficult questions, or even questions they might not feel comfortable asking their own parents. Teachers must remember that they might be the most significant Christian adult in the lives of some of their children. They must never assume that parents are going to deal with questions related to salvation. When these questions arise, teachers must be willing to deal with them personally, without referring them to a pastor or other staff member.

Once children make that commitment to Christ, they need to learn that Christ is a real, living Presence in their lives. They need to understand that He is alive and can help them with their daily challenges. I recently posed this question to my fifth-grade boys who had just finished their lesson on the resurrection. *What personal evidence do you have that Jesus is alive and is part of your life?* One boy responded by saying that he knew that truth from the Bible. Another said, *That's what my parents told me, and they've never lied to me.* I commended the boy on his trust in his parents, but pointed out that he might have friends with parents they trust who might have told them exactly the opposite. I restated my question: *What personal evidence do you have that Jesus is alive and is part of your life?* Aaron thought, then responded by sharing three recent experiences of finding himself in a difficult if not impossible situation. Each time, he prayed; and each time God showed him exactly what to do to get through the difficulty. Children need to make the connection between the truths we teach them each week and the challenges they face each day.

**Youth: Commitments to last a lifetime** – The period of time between ages twelve and eighteen is one of astounding development in practically every area. It is also a time known as *adolescence*, that period between childhood and adulthood that is all but unknown in some cultures. In our culture, adolescence provides a time for adjustment to physiological and psychological changes, for arriving at a degree of self-understanding, for making decisions that affect the future, and for making life commitments. Adolescence affords a protective period during which the teenager can learn, develop, experiment, and decide, usually without the burden of adult responsibilities. Adolescence affords a time of transition and an opportunity for transformation in numerous areas of life.[12]

**Biblical knowledge: superficial to vital.--** A number of years ago I had a conversation with my twelve-year-old son about Sunday School. He was *bored out of his mind*, to use his words. It wasn't the Bible he was bored with. In fact, he spent a lot of time at home reading the Bible. Our nightly father-son bedtime routine had for years involved prayer and a discussion of a Bible verse or passage. His main complaint about Sunday School was, *they teach us the same stories over and over in the same way.* I don't think my son was all that unusual in his attitude toward Sunday School, except that he was willing to openly share his feelings. We tend to teach our children to respect authority and obey parents and teachers. Because of this, they are at times reluctant to share their true feelings. Children who have known the Bible only superficially tend to take that superficiality with them into adolescence. During their teenage years they need to realize it was never the Bible that was boring in the first place; they just had some boring teachers. They need to come to understand what the Bible means and what its principles and teachings mean to them. They need to learn of its relevance. They need to see Jesus for who He is: not the robed, pale-skinned, bearded figure holding either a child or a lamb in a teaching picture, but as an olive-skinned outdoorsman healing a leper, talking with the woman at the well, or driving the money changers from the Temple. My son, now a young adult and a Christian recording artist and performer with a ministry to the younger members of Generation-X, gave me this insight: *Dad, most of my generation would reject the Sunday School image of Jesus I grew up with. They would fall in love with the real Jesus if they had a chance to meet Him.* Youth workers are needed who can awaken youth to the relevance of Scripture and to a very real Jesus that they can fall in love with.

**Faith: from inherited to personal, and from accepting to questioning.--** My family physician when I was a child was the son of a well-known Baptist pastor and the grandson of one of the founders of Southwestern Seminary. He shared in his testimony that as a teenager he came to the point of realizing that he couldn't get to heaven by climbing the "family tree." Many teenagers have grown up in homes where faith in Christ came naturally, and at least partially because of parental influence.

> *Many young members of Generation-X would reject the "Sunday School" image of Jesus. They would fall in love with the real Jesus if they ever had the opportunity to meet Him.*

The time must come, however, when the inherited or "borrowed" faith of childhood must become the very personal and real faith of adolescence and adulthood. This need coincides with another transition during adolescence: from a period of trusting their parents and other authority figures, usually accepting the things they say and do without question, to a period of questioning authority. This is very much related to the young person's growing ability to exercise abstract thinking and critical reasoning and to determine for himself what is right or wrong. Questioning can move

> *Hands-off guidance: Guidance shown to adolescents by teachers, parents, and adult friends through exemplifying the desired behavior and trusting in God and in the adolescent for that needed change.*

over into the faith realm, and this can actually be very healthy. Questioning can bring about that very transition mentioned above – from a borrowed to a personal faith. Youth during this difficult period need understanding, patience, honest answers to questions, "hands-off guidance", and a great deal of prayer.

**Guidance system: from parental control to peer-influence to God-control.--** The shift from parental control to peer influence is going to come naturally. The difficulty lies with the second part of the transition. I trusted Christ as my Savior when I was nine years old. Though I had a fuzzy concept of Christ's Lordship, the adults who helped me through my decision didn't really discuss Christ's Lordship with me. The conscious challenge for me to surrender my to Christ's Lordship came five years later. It was a challenge that as a teenager I could fully understand and accept. It is really not enough for an adolescent to have a growing understanding of Scripture and its teachings. There must come a time when he is willing for those teachings to totally re-order his life, his desires, his thoughts, his actions, and his commitments. Youth need teachers and leaders who exemplify radical obedience to Christ, they need to be confronted with the need to yield to His Lordship, and they need prayer.

**Relationships: from clique to compassion.--** During the period of rapid changes accompanying early adolescence, close exclusive circles of friends (otherwise known as cliques) afford a measure of protection and security. There are two problems with this very natural phenomena: *First,* cliques include some and *exclude others.* Some will always be on the outside and will seldom experience the acceptance of peers during this crucial time. Youth leaders need to be especially sensitive to the needs of those on the outside and work to build for them an environment of acceptance. *Second*, cliques outlast their usefulness. Cliques tend to hang on long past the awkward self-consciousness of the thirteen-year-old and well into the time when Christ, as Lord, expects from teen-age disciples a growing compassion for those who are outside the fellowship of faith. This is one of the most difficult transitions of all, one that will pose immense challenges for youth leaders.

**Adults: Showing Christ to a lost world** – Much has been said already about the need of adults for Bible study that can transform their lives. Review the *costs to be paid by members and staff* and the *Ministry Comparison Chart* (Figure 2) in Chapter 2. Our purpose here is to take a closer look at what might be at the heart of the problem, then to examine possible remedies.

**First, there is the need to bring Bible study to a third level.--** The real problem in our weekly Bible study program might not be that it lacks *depth,* rather, that it lacks *breadth.* Paul, in Acts 19, had just begun a two-year teaching ministry in Ephesus. He started with a small group of converts meeting in a Jewish synagogue. Because of opposition from the Jews as well as the numerical growth of the group, he moved his classes to a public forum – the lecture hall of Tyrannus. There he taught and reasoned with believers on a daily basis. *And this went on for two years, so that all the inhabitants of the province of Asia, both Jews and Greeks, heard the word of the Lord.* (Acts 19:10, HCSB) *This is the third level of Bible study.* Paul's disciples in Ephesus could not simply take in the biblical truths and spiritual insights they were gaining; they had to share them. Remember the Ministry Comparison Chart (Figure 2)? I have shown that chart to hundreds of persons in leadership conferences and in classrooms over the past half-dozen years. A typical response is *Yes, I'll admit that my church is more like the Scribes and Pharisees than Jesus. Unfortunately, nothing can be done.* Many adults have allowed a hollow *cultural Christianity* to replace the real thing.

> **Three Levels of Bible Study**
>
> **Level 1:** Understanding the meaning of a Scripture passage.
> **Level 2:** Deriving *personal* meaning from a Scripture passage.
> **Level 3:** Allowing the impact of that Scripture passage to re-order your life.

**Second, there is the need for church activities to diminish in importance and the indwelling presence of Christ to increase in importance.--** One friend recently put it this way: *Before a person prays to receive Christ, his attention is focused on Christ by those who are trying to lead and guide him in this commitment. After the salvation experience, the focus is no longer on Christ and his need to walk daily with Him, but on the church and its complex program of activities.* Does this sound like a form of idolatry to you, too? Isn't it true that we select Sunday School workers on the basis of their church activity record rather than on their real growth as a disciple? The early church selected Stephen, Philip, and five other "deacons" *not* on the basis of their marital status or whether or not they had ever touched a glass of wine, but on the basis of their reputation as believers, their Spirit-controlled lives, and their spiritual wisdom (Acts 6:3). Haven't we somehow turned this around?

> *The Christian faith is all about the indwelling presence of Christ, not about the institutional church and its program of activities. To believe and practice otherwise is to commit an insidious form of idolatry.*

Adults need teachers who are first of all obedient disciples of a living Christ and who consistently take personal Bible study to that third level. They need teachers and leaders who *get it.* In fact, they need them more than they need a teacher for every twenty-five adults enrolled if those teachers don't know what *it* is.

⬅ *If this paragraph doesn't make sense on the first reading, please read it again.*

Adults need teachers who have first of all allowed Scripture to re-order their own lives, then who will make it will it a matter of utmost importance to convey this vital and essential part of the Christian faith to their learners. Finally, adult learners need to hear Jesus' words, *Not everyone who says to Me "Lord, Lord!" will enter the kingdom of heaven, but the one who does the will of My Father in heaven.* (Matthew 7:21, HCSB). They need opportunities to discover and develop their spiritual gifts, and they need opportunities and encouragement to exercise them.

## *Blended ministry*

It has been true up to this point that one of the primary differences between off-campus, non-traditional Bible study approaches and on-campus approaches is the greater diversity of needs within the unchurched community. The same is true regarding selection of curriculum and purposes in teaching. Within the unchurched community, wide differences in culture, socio-economic level, race, language, and even Christian experience may be found.

It is incorrect to stereotype culturally-different unchurched individuals as being without Christ or a concept of who Christ really is. While that may be generally true, factors other than a lack of Christian faith may explain the unchurched status of those in non-traditional settings. It is not uncommon for unchurched persons to have had a genuine faith experience as a child or as a young person. More recently, they might have felt rejection in a church and simply dropped out. A divorce or other change in family relationships such as a marriage to a non-believer could explain their lack of church participation. It might be that there is no Christian fellowship with which they feel comfortable. It is essential that those who would seek to reach and teach unchurched persons within their community settings first get to know their needs.

**Curriculum: What's appropriate?** That question depends very much on the nature of the group to be reached. Just as in the traditional church, curriculum selection is needs-based. In an Outreach Bible Study fellowship targeting lost persons or individuals who have had no contact with the Bible since their childhood, begin with a very simple curriculum plan that can provide basic information about Christ that in turn can lead to a salvation experience. Brian Robinson, Mission Service Corps volunteer in Amarillo, Texas, was frustrated using traditional Sunday School materials with apartment residents who might be there only a few months. *When we spend their six months in the minor prophets, we may not accomplish a great deal.*[13]

A survey of the mainstream publishers of Bible study materials will very likely reveal a dearth of materials written expressly for persons with little knowledge of Christ. An exception to this would be materials written for other language groups, such as those distributed by Casa Bautista de Publicaciones (Spanish Baptist Publishing House) in El Paso, Texas.[14]

Many have felt the necessity of developing their own curriculum. Mission Arlington has developed the Life of Christ Children's Curriculum that is designed to teach preschoolers through fifth graders the fundamentals of Jesus' life. Topics include the Promise of Advent," "Why Be a Christian?" "How to Become a Christian," When Can I Become a Christian?" "How Does Jesus Become the Boss?" and "Can Jesus Ever Leave My Heart?"[15] Mission Arlington has developed curricula for other ages as well.

Figure 39 to the right gives suggestions for developing curriculum materials for missions settings.

Quite often, standard curriculum materials may be used, particularly when learners demonstrate rapid growth in their faith. Charles Davenport reports that he uses the same Bible study materials in his prison-based class that he does on the main church campus. *The difference*, he indicates, *is that the prisoners study their lessons thoroughly and ask thought-provoking, intelligent questions.*

**Figure 39**
**Keys to Curriculum Development in Missions Settings**

1. Keep it simple and basic, appropriate to the educational level and experience of learners.

2. Keep it sequential, beginning with these fundamentals of the Christian faith:
   - Jesus – His life and atonement
   - Assurance of salvation
   - Basics of the Christian life

3. Keep it relevant and applicable. Help learners to know that the Bible addresses their life needs.

4. Provide for growth beyond the basics as believers mature in their faith.

**The Objective – Making Disciples** The primary difference between Bible study in traditional and non-traditional settings is not necessarily where the learners end; it is often where they begin. Christ can and will transform the lives of those who earnestly seek Him through Bible study. Consider these principles:

- **Blend ministry and Bible study.** See Chapter 9 for a further discussion of outreach, evangelism, and ministry.

- **Be culturally relevant and needs-oriented.** In Bible study, begin as Jesus did -- by meeting the learner where he was, in his life situation.

- **Be purposefully evangelistic.** In traditional Southern Baptist Sunday School materials, there will be on the average four evangelistic lessons per year.[16] It could be more helpful to begin with four evangelistic lessons per month.

- **Teach Christ, not Christian culture.** Christ demands obedience; Christian culture allows for lack of responsibility. Never allow new believers in a missions setting to learn that many Christians do not focus on Christ, merely on "church."

- **Involve new believers in ministry.** Allow them to learn as they serve, and allow service to begin as soon as there is assurance of salvation.

## Notes

# Endnotes

1. LifeWay <u>Church</u> Resources is a division of LifeWay <u>Christian</u> Resources, formerly known as the Baptist Sunday School Board. LifeWay Church Resources is the publishing arm of the agency, and is responsible for Sunday School and Discipleship Training curriculum, LifeWay Press books and materials, Genevox church music, and Broadman/Holman Publishers (academic and trade books) and Holman Bible Publishers.

2. Adapted from Howard P. Colson and Raymond M. Rigdon, *Understanding Your Church's Curriculum*. (Nashville: Broadman Press, 1981), p. 50.

3. Ibid., p. 46.

4. The curriculum publishers in this chart were selected for the following reasons: [1] They are conservative and evangelical in their theology, [2] They are well known by most Christian educators, [3] They have web sites. The web site information is correct as of the date of publication of this book, and may or may not be correct after that.

5. Thomas Sanders and Mary Ann Bradberry, *Teaching Preschoolers: First Steps Toward Faith*. (Nashville: LifeWay Press, 2000), p. 8.

6. Ibid, pp. 14-15.

7. Ibid.

8. Adapted from Sanders and Bradberry, pp. 21-22.

9. This section is adapted from Chris Ward, David Morrow, and Anne Tonks, *Teaching Children: Laying a Foundation for Faith*. (Nashville: LifeWay Press, 2000), pp. 34-35.

10. *Bible Drill* is a Southern Baptist program for older children which helps them to memorize Scripture and learn many Bible facts. *Bible Buddies* is a preparatory program for younger children. LifeWay offers along with children's Sunday School age-appropriate Scripture memorization plans. Scripture memory is part of other Southern Baptist programs such as Royal Ambassadors. AWANA is a Scripture memory club used in many Baptist churches, although it is not Southern Baptist in origin.

11. Adapted from Ward, Morrow, and Tonks, pp. 138-139.

12. Help for this section was received from Chuck Gartman and Richard Barnes in *Youth Sunday School for a New Century*. (Nashville: LifeWay Press, 1999), pp. 20-21.

13. From a conversation with Brian Robinson, Mission Service Corps Volunteer, South Georgia Baptist Church, Amarillo, Texas, on July 23, 2001.

14. The Spanish Baptist Publishing House may be contacted at Casa Bautista de Publicaciones, P.O. Box 4255, El Paso, TX 79914, (800) 755-5958 Orders, (915) 566-9656 Voice, or through their web site, http://www.casabautista.org. English language help is available.

15. From http://www.missionarlington.org/Curriculum.htm

16. From the writers' observation as a curriculum writer for the Baptist Sunday School Board / LifeWay Church Resources over the past 12 years. Every quarter of material has a designated evangelistic lesson. In addition, the inside front cover of every teacher's book and pupil's book contains the plan of salvation.

# Chapter 9
## Getting to Work:  Outreach, Evangelism, and Ministry

Jesus told parables.  Let's try one.

**The Parable of the Baseball Team.--** There was once a very good baseball team.  Their sponsor provided the best equipment on the market. They were particularly proud of their uniforms.  They had an excellent practice field that they used regularly.  They even had an excellent coaching staff.  Each team member had a rule book that he studied individually.  In team meetings they would discuss the rules and talk about strategy.  They especially enjoyed the fellowship on the team. The players and their families enjoyed being with each other on and off the field.  There was only one problem:  *They never played a game.* When asked about this deficiency, the team manager simply said, *An occasional game would be nice, but we really don't have the time with all the practices and team meetings we have.  Besides, we don't play baseball to win games – we just enjoy being a team.*

> *Do these parables sound familiar?  If so, why? How does your Sunday School resemble the baseball team?  The factory?*

Or, consider this one:

**The Parable of the Factory.--** There was once a factory, renowned for the production of lubricating oil.  The factory had won many awards for quality and was well-known throughout the lubricating oil industry.

The factory periodically conducted tours.  A man went on the tour one fine day.  The tour began in the orientation room where the production of oil was explained.  He was shown the room where scientists in their white lab coats developed the formulas to produce the award-winning lubricating oil.  Next, he saw the training room where workers learned to operate the machinery; their diplomas lined the walls.  One of the tour highlights was the room containing the very complex and expensive production machinery.

The tour lasted several hours.  After it was finished, the guide asked if there were any questions.  The man was hesitant at first, but his curiosity finally got the best of him.  *Perhaps I just missed this,* he said, *but I was wondering: How do you ship the oil out?  I didn't see any loading docks or railroad tracks or even pipe lines.*

The tour guide hesitated a minute, then finally admitted: *I'm afraid you've put your finger on a problem that has always confounded our scientists and engineers. You see, it takes all the oil we can produce to keep our own machinery running.*

This chapter deals with getting in the game and going after real opponents, and with sharing our product with the "squeaky" world around us. Outreach, evangelism, and ministry are the means by which we do these things. *Shouldn't these be dealt with in separate chapters?* I believe not. The closer we look at people who need to be reached, the more we see people who are lost. The closer we look at practical evangelism in a hurting world, the more we see the necessity for ministry. Jesus didn't try to separate them into distinct "programs," and neither should we. We will, however, examine the components before putting them together.

## *The Sunday School and outreach*

Earlier you read the story of a church that had declined sharply in attendance over a ten-year period before I began serving as minister of education. Sunday School attendance had dropped an average of 100 per year over that period of time. During my second year there, the downward trend halted and the Sunday School actually grew by a modest amount. It continued growing after I left to begin teaching in a university classroom. The reason for the turn-around? *Outreach.* For the first time, members began getting out in significant numbers to knock on doors and invite others to attend. People were won to Christ through this effort. Church members became more aware of needs within the community for ministry. The old, traditional inner-city church had begun to take on signs of life.

> **Four Phases of an Outreach Program**
>
> *1. Prospect Discovery*
> *2. Prospect Cultivation*
> *3. Prospect Enlistment*
> *4. New Member Assimilation*

Deliberate, planned outreach is a very important key to growth, evangelism, and ministry. Through outreach, we learn of needs for both evangelism and ministry. Through outreach, the church actually begins to be the body of Christ doing the things that Christ would do if He were here in person. Outreach, however, does not just happen. Let's examine the process of reaching people through regular visitation. The process generally involves four phases, the first of which was examined more fully in Chapter 3.

**1. Prospect Discovery.--** A Sunday School prospect is any individual who is not presently involved in Bible study. From Chapter 3, pages 43 through 46, review the methods suggested for discovering prospects including the People Search (Figure 4). Note that some of the methods listed involved the awareness of the person being "discovered" and some methods did not. Recall the importance of safeguarding the information discovered and of making that information part of a prospect file. Recall also that a prospect need not have any real interest in your Bible study program or in your church. Finally, remember that in instances where the individual knows that he has been "discovered," as through a People Search, follow-up must come quickly to be effective.

**2. Prospect Cultivation.--** During this period of time, an unchurched person is brought from the point of no interest or very little interest in Bible study to the point of at least partially seeing its value. While recognition of the need for Bible study falls short of making a real commitment, progress is nevertheless being made. Much patience is required. Ministry needs may be discovered during this process. If so, they must be addressed. This is a time of building bridges and of tearing down barriers. Misconceptions must be cleared up, and communication must be established. Genuine concern must be expressed. Above all, the process must be bathed in prayer. During this time, the greater need in the unchurched person's life may be for a salvation experience.

I'm not a hunter, but I do know the difference between hunting with a shotgun and with a rifle. With a shotgun, you may be trying to "scare something up." You may aim at a flock of birds on the wing and hope to hit something. If, on the other hand, your target is definite and significant (large game), a rifle is called for.

*Do you, in your visitation program, take the shotgun approach or the rifle approach? What is the difference?*

In visitation, we often use the "shotgun" approach. By that, I mean that we take a handful of cards with the names of people we probably don't know. We go out and try to "hit something." If we happen to go out the following week, it's probably to visit someone else. I began to discover the value of using a "rifle" instead of a "shotgun." With the "rifle," you go out with a deliberate "target." The approach was called **TeamReach.**[1] We had just conducted a People Search in which we discovered twenty unchurched family units that could be reached. In most of those families there were one or more lost people. Our survey information was detailed enough to allow us to draw up a profile of each family unit. We enlisted a team of three church members for each of these twenty prospective families, focusing attention on them over a period of six weeks. Each week, the three-member team would meet to pray for their family and would make a contact into the home, generally two-by-two. Team members were selected on the basis of a possible connection with someone in that family. Each week, I would meet with the team leaders of the twenty teams for prayer, evangelism training, and discussion of problems that might have arisen. It became our goal to seek an opportunity to share the gospel in that home by the fourth week and to invite that family to our revival that would take place at the end of the sixth week. Victories were won in that revival, as some twenty adults professed their faith in Christ. The outreach team then became the evangelistic follow-up team in many instances.

In the same church, I learned the hard way not to assume that Sunday School leaders and members knew how to make a visit. In that church, most did not simply because they had never tried. I was walking down the hallway near one of the senior adult departments. I had made it my practice to carry a few prospect cards in my coat pocket, so I was prepared when the president of the Business Women's Class approached me. (The Business Women were in their late sixties and had been "retired" twenty years or more.) *We voted in our last class business meeting to accept a prospect. Do you know one?* I resisted the impulse to comment that prospects didn't really have to be accepted. Instead, I commended her class and replied that I had two names of women about their age that could be contacted. I thought for a moment that the class president would have to call an emergency meeting to accept the second card, but she went ahead and took both. We agreed to touch base in two weeks to see how things had gone.

Two weeks later, I was walking down the same hallway and spotted the president of the Business Women. *How did your visits go?* I asked innocently. *Brother Bob, it was horrible. We'll never try that again.* I asked what the problem seemed to be. *Well, Ethel and I went to the first house. The woman mentioned on that card wasn't home so we just had to throw the card away.* I resisted another urge then asked about the second. *It was even worse*, she replied. I was more than a bit curious by this time. *We went to the home of a Mrs. Green. Brother Bob, would you believe she came to the door wearing a common house dress?* I feigned shock, then asked what happened next. The conversation went something like this:

Pres: *I understand you're a prospect for the Business Women's class.*
Mrs .G: *No, I don't believe I am.*
Pres: *It says on this card that you're a prospect for the Business Women's class.*
Mrs. G.: *I've never heard of the Business Women's Class.*
Pres.: *Our Minister of Education said that you are a prospect for the Business Women's Class.*
Mrs. G.: *I'm sure I don't know your Minister of Education, either.*

And so the conversation went. The two visitors/screening committee members from the Business Women's class tried for five to ten minutes to convince Mrs. Green of her esteemed status as a prospect for their class.

As far as I can tell, the only good thing they did was to keep the name of their church out of the conversation.

To avoid confrontations between well-meaning church members and hapless prospects, provide a combination of classroom orientation and on-the-job training. Include in the orientation sessions suggestions for engaging people in conversation, cultural awareness, when to end the visit, and when and how to share the gospel. Stress the importance of leaving the door open for a follow-up visit.

**3. Prospect Enlistment.--** This should be the most familiar phase of an outreach program, because it's where most outreach is done. The enlistment phase begins at the point of some interest on the part of the prospect and ends with a commitment to become part of your church or your Bible study fellowship. Frequently, these are the people who are "church-hunting." They usually come to us first. They are often Christians, and even Baptists, who have moved into the community and who are looking for a friendly, Bible-believing church with a "good program." I have observed over the years that most of our new members seem to come from this group. It's easy to win this group, but it's often easy to lose them, too.

*Which phase of the outreach program accounts for most of the visits made by your members? How could you achieve a greater degree of balance?*

Other prospects may have reached this phase only after much hard work on the part of a committed outreach or evangelism team. These may be non-believers, new believers, or "back-sliders." After a dozen or so visits into their home and a very tentative commitment to visit one time "just to see," we certainly don't want to blow it. One bad experience can undo the work of several months. Consider the following suggestions for making a good impression on guests:

## Figure 40
## Ten Ways to Make a Good Impression

1. **Refer to new people as *guests*, not *visitors*.** Say, *"We're happy to have you as our guest today,"* rather than *"We're glad you visited."* *Visitor* emphasizes the distance between them and us. *Guest* is a term which honors them and conveys their importance to us. *Visitor* tends to keep new people at arm's length; *guest* implies that they are wanted as part of the family.

2. **Provide guest parking spaces** near the main entrance to the building. This parking area should be clearly marked and indicated from driveway entrances, if there are multiple entrances.

*Continued from the previous page*

3. **Greeters should watch the parking lots** and should give special attention to guests. In rainy weather, provide large umbrellas. My church upon request provides valet parking for senior adults who are not able to find a close spot.

4. **Guests should be directed to the welcome center**, and the center should be clearly indicated from the outside of the building. At the Welcome Center, guests should be asked to register – *but only once.* Copies of their registration card will be taken to the appropriate Sunday School departments. At the guest registration center, information sheets are given stating service and program times, along with a brief message of greeting from the pastor. Maps or diagrams of the building showing locations of various rooms should be available as well.

5. **Volunteers escort families** to their various departments or classes, beginning with the youngest. The volunteers "hand off" members of the family to department directors or greeters along with a copy of the registration information. *Note: Young preschoolers or babies will generally need to be registered separately; parents will generally be asked for additional information.* Some churches provide pagers for parents of younger preschoolers to carry during Sunday School and worship. This can be a great source of comfort, particularly when the children are in a strange environment. If the children are older, volunteer hosts and hostesses will help suggest a meeting place for families.

6. **Guests are greeted in their departments or classes** by the director, outreach leader, or greeter. They are introduced to members with whom they can sit and attend a class. It may be appropriate for nearby members to introduce their new friends.

7. **Guests are escorted into their Sunday School classes** by the new friends they have just met. These individuals see to it that they are introduced to members of the class and that they have copies of the study materials.

8. **Guests are then taken to the worship service** by class members or are taken to pick up or rendezvous with their children.

9. During the welcome time in the worship service, **members should stand while guests remain seated.**

10. **All guests should receive at least two follow-up contacts** during the next week, and at least one of those should be an in-house visit from a Sunday School class leader or member, or from a church staff member.

If it seems that guests should be treated like children who need constant attention, *it is because guests are very much like children who need constant attention!* They can get lost easily, and they can even wander off never to return. We don't want to smother them, but we do want them to feel that their presence is very important to us. We want to be sensitive to their needs at every point. Learn to see your church -- its lay-out, its buildings, its classes, and its fellowship -- as new people would see it for the first time.

> *Three important "Don'ts"*
> 1. *Don't embarrass guests*
> 2. *Don't ignore guests*
> 3. *Don't lose guests*

**4. New member assimilation.--** Two friends were talking across the back yard fence. Both had been annoyed by the constant barrage of Monday night visits from the Baptist church nearby. *I solved the problem*, one friend said. *What on earth did you do?* the neighbor asked. *It's simple*, his friend replied. *I joined that church about three weeks ago, and I haven't heard from them since!*

Everyone needs friends. Sociologists tell us that a normally adjusted adult needs ten or so fairly good friendships. Beyond this circle of friends, there is generally not a felt need to include others as close friends. These "fairly close" friendships would be with people seen frequently in places such as church, clubs, or the workplace. These are the people with whom you visit, exchange Christmas cards, talk on the phone, or enjoy recreational activities. For many adults who are active in church activities, those friendships usually exist within the adult Sunday School class. At this point, we have a strategic problem: People who are new members of adult Sunday School classes are generally in need of new friendships. Perhaps they have moved from another community and have left their old circle of friends behind. Perhaps they have recently received Christ, and they no longer feel close to their old "drinking buddies." Here's the real difficulty: *Those who desperately need new friendships expect to get them in a place where no one else feels the need for any.*

> *What would the visitor in this class be thinking? Do you believe he would return?*

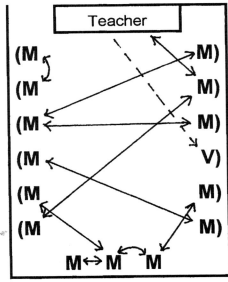

M = Member
V = Visitor

Examine carefully the lines of conversation in the diagram to the right. What problems do you see? How would the visitor feel? How could members be led to be more sensitive? What specific actions could be taken to alleviate the problems?

The process of new member assimilation begins when a person visits a class for the first time. That new person must see potential new friends within the class. The process continues when that person joins. It continues well into the period that the new member is ready and willing to serve. Consider the following actions to help assimilate new members:

**Actions Taken Within the Class:** Begin developing a relationship with prospective members when the visit or when the first contact is made into their home. Consider the following on-going actions:

- Train class members in their understanding of the needs of new people for friendships, and remind them of the dangers of losing people who feel that they are not making friends in the class.

- Assign each new member to be part of a care group, with frequent contacts coming from that care group leader. The care group leader should lead out in the assimilation process in the class.

- Appoint a mentor for each new member. This person might or might not be the care group leader. This could be a discipleship partner for a new believer. For an experienced Christian, the mentor should be someone who would help him to establish "networks" within the church.

## Figure 40
## Strategies for Welcoming New Members

| Strategy #1 | Strategy #2: |
|---|---|
| When the new member joins, he should immediately be presented to the church as a new member. This is true whether he is a new believer or whether he has been a Christian for many years and has recently moved to the community. This will give people in the congregation an opportunity to come by and greet the new member. We should assume that this person is sincere and has made a solid commitment. He will probably become part of a Sunday School class, but that should be left entirely to the individual. When he has been an active member for several years, he will probably come to the attention of the nominating committee and will be considered for a service job in the church. | When a new member joins, he should be taken immediately to a counseling room. The trained counselor will immediately help the new member to be sure of his conversion experience (this is true even for persons moving their membership). He then will be given the name of his Sunday School teacher and should expect a contact during the week from this individual. The counselor or another assigned person will serve as a mentor over the new few weeks, seeing that the new member becomes involved in an adult class, that he receives training for new Christians or new church members, and that he comes to an awareness of his spiritual gifts. He will probably be presented to the congregation on Sunday evening or the following Sunday morning. |

*Which of the above strategies is best? Why?*

- Involve the new member in service opportunities as quickly as possible. These might include visitation, being part of an evangelism team, or singing in the choir.

**Actions Taken Within the Church:** Just as in the Sunday School class, the process of assimilation of new church members begins with their first visit to the church or with the first contact into their homes. Allow your interest in them to be genuine. Provide the information they need concerning the church, its ministries, and its members. Consider taking several of these actions at the time they join:

- When the new members are presented to the church, invite members of their Sunday School classes to stand with them as they are greeted by the congregation.

- As an alternative to asking them to stand at the front of the church at the end of the service, have a brief reception for new members.

- Consider a monthly fellowship honoring new members.

- Invite all new members to complete a talent and interest survey to determine their service experience, interests, and availability.

- Consider taking those who present themselves for membership into a counseling room where several things will take place: Their commitment to Christ will be "nailed down." They will be assigned a mentor to disciple them or help them establish friendships within the church. They will be given the name of their Sunday School teacher. They will be assigned to a new members' class. Finally, they will be presented to the church at a later time.

- As an alternative, assign a senior staff member or a trained deacon (or deacon's wife) to each new member to assess their needs and help them to take the next steps toward growth, Christlikeness, and service.

**Leading members to participate in outreach.** The records speak for themselves in most churches. Relatively few otherwise involved Christians ever make a visit to a lost or unchurched person. Participation by a significant number of members in activities to reach lost and unchurched people is an essential part of growth. A

*Planned Outreach* – organized efforts to involve a significant number of Sunday School members in planned outreach activities directed toward the lost and unchurched population of the community.

*Lifestyle Outreach* – unplanned, unstructured efforts on the part of committed Christians to invite their friends, relatives, co-workers, and neighbors to join them in Bible study.

rule of thumb is that at least 10% of the active Sunday School attendance should be involved each week in outreach. A combination of "planned outreach" and "lifestyle outreach" approaches should be used.

**Planned Outreach Activities.--** The heart of this strategy is regular, weekly visitation. There are many advantages to having a regular time and place for visitation. Many churches plan visitation on Monday evenings following a light supper. For older adults and retirees, a weekday morning time could be planned. As has been mentioned, outreach assignments should be made at Wednesday night Sunday School planning meetings for visits to be made on the way home. Outreach events are usually not difficult to plan and promote. Why, then, do relatively few participate? Consider these reasons:

1. **Lack of expectation.--** As pastors and staff leaders, we generally treat outreach as an optional activity only for the super-committed. We really don't expect most members to participate. For many years, North Phoenix Baptist Church, under the leadership of its pastor and senior staff, made it clear that participation in activities to reach the lost was part of the normal Christian life of every member. As a result, hundreds participated each week, and North Phoenix became one of the fastest growing Southern Baptist Churches. An ideal time to express this expectation to members is *before* they join.

2. **Lack of leadership.--** Someone has to be in charge of outreach. In multi-staff churches, this person would generally be the minister of education or minister of outreach and evangelism. For many churches, the Sunday School Outreach/Evangelism Director would give leadership to the ministry. This individual directs the enlistment and training of outreach leadership throughout the Sunday School, supervises the preparation of prospect assignments, and leads out in promoting the outreach events.

3. **Lack of an organization.--** The Outreach/Evangelism Director can't do everything that needs to be done. Within every department and every adult and youth class there must be an outreach/evangelism leader who meets regularly with the Sunday School Outreach/ Evangelism Director and who enlists persons in his class or department to participate.

4. **Lack of preparation.--** Many outreach approaches will succeed or fail based on the quantity and quality of prospect information available for assignment. It would help most visitation teams to know that the information on their assignment card is accurate and up-to-date. It would be helpful to know how the information was obtained. (Did this individual visit the church or was his name obtained in a People

Search?) Information about family members would be helpful, as well as results of previous visits. The preparation of this information could be a major responsibility of a church secretary or of an outreach secretary with a great deal of time to commit. Other things that should be prepared ahead of time include information sheets about the church, maps, witnessing tracts, and the assignment room itself.

**Lifestyle outreach.--** This type of outreach is simply one friend inviting another friend to participate in life-changing Bible study. The "friend" can also be a neighbor, classmate, co-worker, or relative. Lifestyle outreach works best when:

★ The Bible study to which friends are being invited truly changes lives.

★ Those who participate in this Bible study take seriously their responsibility to make this same life-changing experience available to others.

## *The Sunday School and evangelism*

One Sunday I gave a "pop test" to a fifth grade boy who was very active in Sunday School. I asked him to pretend that I was a lost person who knew very little about Jesus. He had only two minutes to tell me about Jesus, His plan of salvation, and what I needed to do in order to be saved. The ten-year-old did a great job with thirty seconds to spare and didn't leave out any of the "important parts." If sharing one's faith is so simple that a fifth grader can do it with no preparation time, why then is it so difficult for most adults to share their faith? Every person who attends a Bible study on a regular basis should be equipped to share his or her faith in Jesus Christ. It's that simple.

Sunday School is the most important evangelistic tool the church has to use in its witness to the community. It has the potential of impacting more lives than any other church ministry. It has the largest group of believers that can be trained and mobilized. It has the necessary resources. It provides a good setting for discipleship and growth of new believers to take place. It is capable of providing fellowship, Bible study, and ministry to relate to its evangelistic efforts. With all this potential, many Sunday Schools have yet to take the challenge of evangelism seriously. In many churches,

> **FAITH Outline**
> F is for Forgiveness
> A is for Available. (Forgiveness is available to all, but it is not automatic)
> I is for Impossible (for God to allow sin into heaven
> T is for Turn (or repent)
> H is for Heaven (here and hereafter)

*Page 159*

evangelism and Bible study maintain two separate tracks. Evangelism, for example, is often carried out as a separate program that is in no way connected with Sunday School outreach efforts. In many evangelism presentation plans, there is no natural method to use in follow-up discipleship. Sunday School at times maintains a "Christian culture" that is largely unaware of either the presence of or the needs of the lost community. It's time for that to change.

**Putting evangelism back in the Sunday School.** FAITH Sunday School Evangelism Strategy, in a growing number of Southern Baptist churches, has done exactly that. FAITH features an easily remembered presentation outline. The primary value of the strategy is in its relationship to the Sunday School rather in the outline itself. Here are some of the basic features of that relationship:[2]

- Evangelism teams are made up of Sunday School class leaders and members.

- Evangelistic visits are actually Sunday School visits with an evangelistic purpose.

- Ideally, the three team members come from the same Sunday School class or department.

- During the visit, one team member shares a testimony of the benefits (spiritual growth, fellowship, practical help) of being in a Sunday School class.

- As a lost person is led to Christ, the Sunday School class then provides the basic nurturing Bible study fellowship that the new Christian needs.

- Evangelism leaders are Sunday School leaders. The term *outreach/evangelism leader* or *FAITH Evangelism leader* is generally used rather that *outreach leader*.

- Evangelism team leaders are provided on-the-job training over a period of several months. Two "trainees" are generally sent out with an experienced witness. These, then, serve as trainers or team leaders as others are enlisted to be on evangelism teams.

FAITH Evangelism Strategy is published by LifeWay Christian Resources. Periodic FAITH regional training clinics are provided in strategic locations around the country throughout the year. More than 5,500 churches and 25,000 individuals have been trained in FAITH through one of the clinics.[3] Before materials can be ordered for a church, it is essential that the senior pastor be trained at one of the regional clinics.

The principles listed above are not limited to use of the FAITH evangelism outline. Rather, they can be used with wide variety of presentation methods such as those in Figure 41. After reviewing these methods, consider additional suggestions listed below for making evangelism more a part of the Sunday School.

### Figure 41
### Evangelism Presentation Methods

| Method | Author/Publisher | Web Address or Contact Information |
|---|---|---|
| 4 Spiritual Laws | Campus Crusade for Christ, International | www.ccci.org |
| Eternal Life | North American Mission Board | www.namb.net (Link to evangelism resources) |
| Evangelism Explosion | D. James Kennedy, Evangelism Explosion International | www.eeinternational.org |
| EvangeCube | Affiliated with Child Evangelism Fellowship International | www.evangecube.org |
| FAITH Sunday School Evangelism Strategy | LifeWay Christian Resources | www.lifeway.com/sundayschool/faith/ |
| Share Jesus Without Fear | William Fay | www.letsgo.org |

- Begin with those who are presently committed to personal evangelism. On each team of three, include one or two inexperienced people.

- If your curriculum includes quarterly evangelistic lessons, maximize the benefit of those lessons by striving to invite several lost persons to attend.

- Provide as much evangelism training as possible during Sunday School lessons that are on a related topic.

- Invite Sunday School class members to share experiences of leading lost persons to Christ.

- Encourage class members to use their natural contacts to share their faith personally or as part of a team effort.

- Be aware of other ministry needs as you make evangelistic contacts, and be ready to help meet those needs.

## *The Sunday School and ministry*

Long before there were class outreach leaders and care group leaders, ministry was very much a part of many if not most Sunday School classes. In churches I've served, it would be difficult to image a serious illness, accident, or death without caring actions being taken by members of the Sunday School class. There's only one problem: Our ministry actions are almost always directed to other believers; they seldom touch unchurched or lost people in the community.

Kathy is a divorcee and mother of two young children. She takes care of her family on the meager income from a part-time job. Her telephone has been shut off, her car has broken down, and it will be a very short time before her utilities are disconnected. Her children need clothes, and food in her house is pretty scarce toward the end of the month. On top of everything, her son has a hyperactive disorder and she has a hard time getting him to the doctor located across town. Kathy is a Christian and wants to be in church with her children. Her problems seem to outweigh her opportunities.

> *What are Kathy's needs? Could you list several actions that could be taken by a church or a single adult Sunday School class to help Kathy and her family?*

Kathy represents many in our communities who could be reached by traditional, on-campus Sunday School classes if some ministry needs could be met along the way. Many churches have used a needs assessment survey in place of the traditional people search as a means of learning about their neighbors. In developing your own survey form, consider these questions:

1. What are some of the needs that you've noticed that people in your community have?

2. In your opinion, what are some ways that ____ Baptist Church could help people in this community?

3. In addition to what you've told us, are there some specific ways that our church could help your family?

4. We'd love to have the opportunity to pray for you and your family. Are there some specific things that we could pray about?

If it would help to solicit a response, you probably could suggest some things that the church already provides or could provide such as parenting classes, divorce recovery classes for adults and children, child care, after school tutoring, a clothes closet, or a food pantry.

> Write a "P" in the blank beside the ministries that your church provides for people in the community. Write a "C" beside ministries that your church should consider. Add other items to the list that would be appropriate in your community.
>
> ___ 1. Food pantry
> ___ 2. Clothes closet
> ___ 3. Van transportation for elderly
> ___ 4. After school tutoring
> _C_ 5. Parenting classes
> _C_ 6. Marriage enrichment classes
> _C_ 7. Divorce recovery classes
> _C_ 8. Free child care (Mothers' Day Out)
> _P_ 9. Bus ministry
> _C_ 10. Literacy classes
> ___ 11. Conversational English classes
> ___ 12. After school recreation

As your Sunday School begins getting out in the community, it will discover many needs for ministry such as those listed above. Some of those ministries will be a means of reaching people for Christ. Some will result in persons being reached for traditional Sunday School classes. Some will be discovered who can be reached only through off-campus Bible study approaches such as those discussed in the *Blended ministry* sections of this book.

## *The Jesus model: putting it all together*

*Outreach, evangelism, ministry. Isn't one as good as the other? Isn't it enough, for example, just to have a good outreach program? Can these three concepts be combined into one ministry? Shouldn't churches specialize in one of these activities?*

These are all very good questions. If we are content simply to do outreach without evangelism, we will probably be looking for Christians who are looking for a church. Certainly, people need to find a church home in their new community, but how does that really impact the

> *In what ways would Jesus' ministry have been different if He had allowed the attitudes of the hometown people at the synagogue in Nazareth to shape it? Are there times that we must be willing to do the unpopular thing in our churches in order to be like Jesus?*

kingdom? If we do outreach without ministry, we tend to reach out to "our kinds of people." One of my early pastors discouraged me from visiting people with financial needs. His reason was, T*hey can't support our church.* The simple truth is that outreach, evangelism, and ministry *must never* be separated. Our model for that style of ministry is Jesus.

When Jesus read from the Isaiah scroll in his home town synagogue, he indicated that much of His ministry would be directed toward *the poor, captives, blind, and oppressed* (Luke 4:18-19). When He did so, the home town people were amazed. When Jesus hinted that His ministry would be in part to the *Gentiles* (vv. 21-27), they were outraged. Recall Jesus' words sent as a message to John the Baptist: *The blind receive their sight, the lame walk, the lepers are cleansed, the deaf hear, the dead are raised, and the poor have good news preached to them* (Luke 7:22b, HCSB). We see Jesus' blend of evangelism and ministry in forgiveness and healing of the lame man (Luke 5:17-24) and in the restoring of sight to the blind man at the pool of Siloam (John 9). We see Jesus in passages such as John 4:1-38 (the woman at the well in Samaria) or John 8:2-11 (the woman caught in the act of adultery) loving the sinner while rejecting the sin. The bottom line is this: *If our Sunday Schools are to be pleasing to Jesus, their members must be led to be like Him.* There's no other way. Perhaps it's time to take our image of Jesus less from the Sunday School pictures and more from the pictures we've just seen.

## *Blended ministry*

The term "social gospel" was not intended as a compliment when it was popularized in the 1970's. The term was used by conservative, evangelical Christians to refer to so-called liberal churches that substituted "wash rags" for Christian witness. The term came out of the perception that social ministry – soup kitchens, homeless shelters, and similar activities – was a substitute for genuine evangelism. For some churches and denominations, that might have been the case. For others, it was simply a way of giving a cup of cold water in Christ's name. Many of the more "conservative" churches reacted to the "social gospel" crowd by practically eliminating ministries to those in need. This trend continues to this day with increasing emphasis on evangelism *(a good thing)* but very little attention given to *the poor, the captives, the blind, and the oppressed (a very bad thing)*. One prominent theological seminary eliminated its school of social work and strengthened its school of evangelism. Other schools have replaced degrees in social work with programs in "church and community ministry."

**Hot gospel or social gospel?** – For many churches, this question is more difficult than it should be. Many see Christ's commissions to evangelize as the mission of the church; nothing else really matters. Some, operating from this perspective, argue that it is the individual and not the church that should be involved in meeting the social needs of people.

For others, it is the church that should address the social concerns. Some would go so far as to score the role of personal evangelism. Their rationale is that conditions such as racism, poverty, and broken homes prevent persons from becoming what God intended them to be. They argue that personal transformation cannot alter the oppressive environments in which people live. Churches must therefore act to correct social injustice and provide a healthy environment.[4]

### Figure 42
### Which Gospel?

| *Hot Gospel:* Evangelism that is devoid of any type of ministry that addresses physical or social concerns of people. It recognizes only their spiritual needs. | *Social Gospel:* Social action that is devoid of evangelism and that wants nothing more than a better world for those in need. It fails to address spiritual needs. |
|---|---|

*Whole Gospel:*
The grace of God through Jesus Christ applied to the whole person; it addresses the spiritual, social, physical, and emotional needs of people.

William Pinson and many others advocate the *whole gospel* approach, combining personal evangelism and Christian nurture with Christian social action.[5] These cannot really be separated. Conversion, Bible study, and prayer not only transform hearts but can also bring about social change. Sobriety, a recommitment to family, and a new work ethic frequently accompany the change within a person's heart. There are times when additional intervention is needed.

**A platform for evangelism.--** Part of the motivation for addressing social concerns is that evangelism can be enabled. Missiologists speak of a *platform for evangelism* as doing whatever is needed to gain a hearing. On the international mission field, the platform might be a medical clinic, a hunger relief program, English classes, or any one of a hundred other things. Platforms for evangelism are frequently needed in communities as well, particularly where a credibility gap exists between the target group and the Christian presence. Governmental and community agencies can and do provide for many social needs for food, clothing, and shelter. Since these actions are seldom connected with faith, they can do little to provide hope for a better life. Neither can governmental or community agencies provide for all the needs that exist. Churches can and must act so as to fill this gap. We must act because there are needs, we must act because we care, and we must act because it's exactly what Christ would do.

Many people who have significant social and economic needs feel a tremendous barrier separating them from organized religion. They see churches as part of the "mainstream" of society and their members as the "haves." They see themselves as the "have-nots," and very definitely out of society's mainstream. They feel that we don't care about them, and tragically, they have a point. They therefore have no compelling reason to listen to our message. *They don't care what we know until they know that we care.*

> *Many people don't care what we know until they know that we care.*

How do we show them that we care? One way is through their children. Don Lane of City Church, Amarillo, observed that the highest compliment he is ever paid by a lost person with social and economic needs is that "You guys really love my children." I've had the same experience. I work with children in my church's low-income neighborhood. Along with other godly men and women I have opportunities to teach them, take them swimming and fishing, and take them on campouts and lock-ins. In the process of participating in these activities, the children learn who Jesus is. For a mature middle-aged man to be willing to spend the night on the floor of a gymnasium, love has got to be involved. Since I love their children, this gives me something in common with parents in the community: we both love their kids. This common ground enables me to go into low-income homes of unchurched people all over town and be called by name and invited to come inside.

Other methods of gaining a hearing include formal surveys, informal conversations, or simply spending time on "their turf." Don Lane found one especially innovative method – one involving thousands of pounds of potatoes. An old traditional Southern Baptist church in a low-income, racially-mixed area of east Amarillo had virtually shut its doors. The church deeded its property to City Church, and a date was set for the launch of the new mission. The week prior to the first Sunday, Don arranged for pickup trucks loaded with more than 5,000 pounds of potatoes to be parked next to the building. The word quickly spread throughout the community that there were free potatoes down at the Baptist church. Volunteers helped sack up the potatoes as they issued invitations to the first service to be held the following Sunday. The old Anglo congregation had averaged around ten to twelve in its last month of existence. Don reported ninety in attendance on the first Sunday of the new work, and in almost two years, that has been the lowest attendance to date.

Showing that you care comes with a price. You can't write a check, and you can't "phone it in." You can't do it from your office, either. You have to be there, and you have to plan to stay for a while.

**A ministry to Jesus.–** Another reason for addressing the social needs of people comes from the words of Jesus:

> *The righteous will answer Him, "Lord, when did we see You hungry and feed You, and thirsty and give You something to drink? When did we see You a stranger and take You in or without clothes and clothe You? When did we see you sick, or in prison, and visit You?" And the King will answer them, "I assure you: Whatever you did for one of the least of these brothers of Mine, you did for Me."* (Matthew 25:37-40, HCSB)

There can be no higher motivation for ministry than this. We don't do it to make *us* feel good. We don't even really do it for *them.* We do it for Jesus. This takes acts of ministry and social concern to a new level. Since we're doing this as an act of devotion to Jesus, it doesn't make sense to look down on the people we're trying to help. Jesus treated people with genuine acceptance and respect; we must as well. He made them feel better, not worse, about themselves; we must as well.

**Are you a missionary or a missions volunteer?–** I learned the distinction between these terms on a half-dozen mission trips to Argentina. Being a missions volunteer is a good thing. You leave your comfort zone and go to a strange and very different place, perhaps in another country. You endure discomfort, and you eat things you never believed you could get down. You then share Christ's love with people who need to hear and watch as God brings about miracles. Then, you pack up and go back home. Your missions experience is over. The missionary, on the other hand, stays. He has found a new home among the people he is serving. He returns to his family and friends in the land of his birth for brief visits. His ministry is incarnational. I've noticed that when missionaries speak of "going home," they're usually on furlough at the time!

There is more to being involved in cross-cultural "whole gospel" ministries in your local mission field than going in for a short time and coming back out, never to return again. Remember, *this is the mission trip that doesn't end.* That doesn't mean you say goodbye and leave your family and friends behind to travel to a distant place. It does, however, mean that you allow yourself to fall in love with people who need the hope that is found in Christ and the help that can come through your church. It means that you keep on going back, week after week. You pay the price to gain acceptance and trust. You become a missionary: an incarnational presence of Christ's love in the midst of a people who need that love.

## Notes


## Endnotes

1. This program of targeted evangelistic visitation was developed by the writer at Rosen Heights Baptist Church of Fort Worth in 1981. It is not to be confused with other programs by that name, at least one of which was developed by the Baptist Sunday School Board (LifeWay).

2. These principles as well as the FAITH outline are from the Faith Evangelism Strategy® training materials published by LifeWay Christian Resources, and made available through regional training clinics.   Contact the FAITH web site for additional information: www.lifeway.com/sundayschool/faith/

3. From the Faith Sunday School Evangelism Strategy web site made available through LifeWay Christian Resources:   http://www.lifeway.com/sundayschool/faith/

4. William M. Pinson, Jr., *Applying the Gospel: Suggestions for Christian Social Action in a Local Church.* (Nashville: Broadman Press, 1975), pp. 77.

5. Ibid.